No Place
To Belong

By
Ann Warren

British Library Cataloguing in Publication Data.
A catalogue record for this book is available from the British Library

ISBN 978 0 86071 679 2

A Commissioned Publication of

MOORLEYS
Print & Publishing
tel: 0115 932 0643 web: www.moorleys.co.uk

Contents

Ann Warren's Previous Publications

~~~~~

Love Letters

Marriage in the Balance

Today's Christian Woman

Facing Bereavement

Living with Unemployment

Happily Ever After

Free to be Myself

Confessions of Annabel Brown aged 59¾

~~~~~

Prologue

Was it possible he could still be alive and, if so, where would I find him now?

So many years had passed since we first knew each other as children. I, the small child who had come to stay with his parents when my mother was dying, and John, my greatly adored big cousin with the deep laugh and the wonderful sense of fun!

I was seven by the time that both my parents died. It was wartime, and because ships were regularly being torpedoed, it was thought unsafe to send me to live with my mother's family in South Africa.

I think that my parents had assumed that John's father would look after me when they died. But although I had often stayed there when my parents were sick, his mother apparently felt she could not possibly cope with another much younger child, and so it was that I was adopted away from the family.

My adoptive parents were resolutely determined to keep away any real flesh and blood relations who tried to stay in touch. I was to become their sole possession and theirs alone. So that now, many years later, tracking down my own real family had proved a long and dusty uphill search against almost impossible odds.

A few years back I had finally succeeded in tracing my mother's family in South Africa.

Meeting up with my family after all those years adrift had felt as if the tent peg of my life had finally slotted into the right shaped hole, giving me an amazing sense of actually 'belonging' for the first time since my parents died. I returned home after that visit desperate to stay in touch with them and wishing with all my heart that they were not so far away.

But tragically, only a few weeks after this extraordinary reunion, my husband Peter had fallen terminally ill with cancer, and this wonderful discovery had faded far into the background as we struggled to fight this terrible disease together during his last few years.

1

Now I was looking for my father's family, I knew that, as my adoptive mother had never tired of telling me, "they had not wanted me", but somewhere deep down I still had this wonderful memory of two much older cousins living in the house where I was not allowed to stay.

Some twenty years earlier Peter and I had found out where they lived and briefly made contact with John and his wife on a business trip to Australia, but they had not stayed in touch and so I had simply assumed that they did not want to know. Was it worth trying again and would the trail have gone cold all these years later?

Almost without thinking I entered my cousin's name and possible location into the Yellow Pages website up on the screen in front of me, and then stopped short with a real sense of shock - there was his name large as life on the screen.

I was staying with my daughter in Sydney at the time and according to Yellow Pages he was now only a few hours away down near Canberra.

I took a deep breath and picked up the phone.

"You will never guess who this is?" I started tentatively, using one of the oldest clichés in the book.

Difficult to be original at such a time!

"I'm afraid you've got the advantage of me there," he said, probably wondering who on earth this stupid woman was.

As we talked, he gradually seemed to take on board who I was, though it felt as if this memory was emerging from a very great depth. Did he really remember me or was he just being polite?

"Why don't you come down to visit me?" he suddenly suggested. "Unfortunately I am confined to base after a stupid car accident, so I can't really get out at the moment, but you could easily come here."

Suddenly, I felt as if this was all getting too close for comfort, experiencing a distinct urge to back away. Quickly, I tried to put the whole idea on hold muttering something about possibly coming down that way sometime if I was able to. But it remained a tempting thought which refused to go away.

When I had finally arranged to meet up with my mother's family in South Africa, my poor husband almost had to drag me to see them when we were practically on the doorstep. I had got cold feet at the very last minute - and now it looked as if exactly the same syndrome was about to repeat itself - but this time there was no one to help me get over the panic.

It seemed extraordinary that this should happen after all those years of dreaming of being reunited with my family, but now, yet again, it felt as if real life was becoming all too risky and substantial.

Dedication

For my children and grandchildren and for all the wonderful
friends who have helped me down the years
and encouraged me in the writing of this book.

Chapter One

The Beginning of the End

The whole sky exploded into brilliant orange sprays of light splattering the dark silhouettes of London faraway on the horizon. Night after night our house shook and echoed with deep resonant thuds heralded by the eerie wail of that sinister siren.

I can remember standing by the open window transfixed by what to a small child seemed like an enchanting firework display laid on for my benefit - and then being whisked down the stairs to hide yet again beneath the imagined safety of the kitchen table.

As stray bombs landed closer and closer to our home my parents obviously decided that it was impossible for us all to go on living there. And like so many other London children in those days, I too had to leave wonderful familiar surroundings - a garden with an old swing, a small black Scotty dog, and delightful neighbours who grew lovely big red tomatoes in their greenhouse. Curious things little children remember.

At least I was lucky in that my parents were able to come away with me and that I was not being shipped off into the blue like so many evacuee children. We moved to Cambridge, taking over part of an old house with a rather fearsome landlady living next door.

My parents seemed to find this whole move really exhausting and stressful. But I was immediately enchanted by the glorious world of lovely old grey stone colleges just down the road, and a river bank thick with willows, where punts glided past and daffodils were sprinkled like a carpet of gold.

But as this exciting new world opened up before me I had no way of knowing that all this would herald the end of my childhood forever. We would never again return to our own home and within three years there would be nothing left of my family to tell the tale.

Just a few faded photographs are left to tell me of that time when I really 'belonged' and when two people obviously cared very deeply for me - but by the time I was seven that world had gone for ever.

My mother seemed to be continuously ill and with the impatience of a small child I longed to be out playing by the river or away with my friends.

School was a Catholic convent just down the road which we walked to every morning, careful not to step on the cracks in the pavement in case the bears got us. The nuns seemed amused by our antics and nothing in the way of school work was very demanding.

I do remember getting into terrible trouble for filling the whole of my new exercise book with what I thought was a truly fascinating story, fully and graphically illustrated. And I never did really understand why they got so upset. Perhaps the ramblings of a compulsive writer had taken over even at that early age!

My mother was about to have a baby and I was supposed to be pleased. It seemed a vaguely dissatisfying thought which became a hundred times worse as I was taken in to see my new brother for the first time. With the curious instinct of a small child I knew immediately that there was something badly wrong with him and I remember backing away in revulsion.

In fact Peter suffered from Downs syndrome and even if they had tried to explain I don't suppose I would have understood. In the next few years I came to love him despite my earlier feelings, but they took him away to live in a home some distance away and I hardly ever saw him.

My mother continued to be constantly sick and tired, but no one ever explained to me what this meant. By this time she was being looked after in a Nursing Home just next door to my school, and I went to visit her every day at break instead of playing with my friends out in the sunshine.

I hated that darkened room where the curtains were always drawn and the silence seemed somehow paralyzing. I wanted to take her away back home to play on the lawn with me and to live a normal life again. It sometimes seemed as if she could hardly speak to me and I became deeply afraid. Everything in me longed to escape back into the normal world of light and laughter.

Then one day she suddenly said to me, "You don't have to come here every day. Why don't you stay and play with your friends in the playground and only come here when you really want to come."

I felt the most enormous sense of release. Had she understood what I was feeling all along? It was as if she had given me permission to live again, and with the blissful ignorance of a small child I immediately accepted her offer. It was to be a decision, and a day, that I would regret for the rest of my life.

Just as we were being called in from break I saw one of the sisters from the Nursing Home talking to the teacher on duty and they called me over. To this day I don't understand why the words were said, but they remain burnt into my memory.

"Whatever were you doing out here playing? Your mother was calling for you just before she died, and we couldn't find you anywhere."

The feeling of guilt was almost overwhelming. With the innocence of a small child I felt as if I had personally been responsible for her death - as if it could have been prevented. If only, if only.

The awareness of death comes slowly to the young and very much alive, but already I felt its sting. I felt numb, detached, and in a place where no one could reach me.

My father tried to help me understand. He would always love me and look after me he said and together we went to see the place where they had buried her. There was no tombstone, nothing but a heap of recently dug soil to show me where they had put her.

Edith was a lifeline for me now. She was the lovely cook housekeeper who looked after us both and waited for me when I came home from school. The warm kitchen where she baked her cakes was a haven to come home to and a place where I could still belong. But the shadows were lengthening still and then my father had to go into hospital for the first time - they said he just seemed to be fading away.

Edith's friend John, in his gorgeous army uniform, appeared more and more regularly in the house. I loved him to bits and was thrilled to hear that they were going to be married - especially since I was to be the bridesmaid. Everything was bustle and excitement as the great day approached.

It was a magic day full of music and colour. Long fingers of sunlight streamed down through the stained glass windows of the lovely old church sprinkling Edith's wedding dress with rainbow-coloured patterns and lighting up the flowers that seemed to be everywhere. The celebrations went on long into the evening with partying and dancing. I remember John dancing with me shoulder high above the crowds and feeling so happy I could almost burst.

As the two of them said goodbye and gave me a long lingering hug, I don't think I still really understood the implications of all that was happening.

The next day as my father and I breakfasted alone, he told me to pack up a few of my belongings and my favourite toys as I was going to have to go away for a while. But after that nothing further was said. We spent that last day alone down by the river watching the punts glide along the banks and people fishing beneath the willows. I recall that he was very silent and seemed reluctant to go home, but it was the evening that was burnt into my mind forever.

As soon as we got home the dreaded suitcase was collected and we set off in the direction of school and the old convent. My father was strangely silent now as if struggling to find the occasional word. I had never seen him like this before and something chill stirred deep within me.

As we came to the dark gravel drive of the convent with its overhanging cedar trees, he stopped at the top of the steps and pulled the rusty iron handle in the wall. His voice sounded choked as he finally found the words, "I am going to have to leave you here."

Footsteps were approaching, and I watched apprehensively as the heavy glass-panelled door opened. A rather shrivelled figure in black gazed down with sad eyes, her crucifix swinging gently somewhere around her waist.

"Ah, so this is the little girl," she said in a kind but rather distant voice as if contemplating a delivery of vegetables.

My father refused her offer to come in, but held back hesitantly.

"You'll be alright here - I know you will," he said. "I'm afraid I have to go. They are expecting me at the hospital."

He hugged me briefly to him, and then almost pushed me inside the door, before stumbling down the steps and off towards the high stone gates of the convent. Shoulders hunched and hands thrust deep into his pockets, I watched despairingly as he didn't even look back to wave goodbye.

I have often wondered what he was feeling in those last desperate moments and why it was that he could not really bring himself to tell me what was happening.

Every step on the harsh black and white marbled floor echoed round the enormous hallway, as I followed Sister Agnes hesitantly towards the staircase. I stole a quick glance back towards the front door in case my father had had second thoughts, but the frosted glass held no familiar comforting shadow.

I felt my eyes stinging with tears as I followed the old nun reluctantly up the well-worn staircase. The whole building seemed silent and unwelcoming. Perhaps it was all some terrible nightmare and I would suddenly wake to find the sun shining and everyone I loved back home around me.

The nun paused to recover her breath at the top of the winding stone staircase, and then led the way along a narrow corridor to the right. Against the wall there were a few upright cupboards hardly wide enough for me to stand in. Sister Agnes peered inside a couple of these and then opened the third. "Put your belongings in here," she commanded, "and be sure they are kept tidy."

The handful of clothes I had packed, together with my much loved teddy bear, seemed to almost rattle in the cupboard with the creaking door and the smell of stale polish.

"Come along," she said, reaching down a bony hand for me to hold onto, "I will show you the dining room where I believe they have put your supper out ready for you."

11

Back down the stone staircase we came to an enormous room full of polished trestle tables and rows and rows of empty places laid in readiness. At the far end in what seemed the darkest corner stood a glass of milk and two pieces of bread "thinly scraped" as Edith would have described them.

"Ah, here it is," said Sister Agnes. "Now sit here quietly and eat your supper. It is time for Chapel now, and afterwards one of the other sisters will show you where you are to sleep."

Scraping the chair back from the table, she scarcely waited for me to sit down before gliding purposefully in the direction of the door.

"But what about the others?" I heard my voice die in the empty air before the door shut firmly on the retreating nun's back.

The silence of the vast dining room was icy cold, and the bread and milk looked the most unappetising meal I had ever seen. Surely this could not really be happening. Maybe if I shut my eyes I would find myself back in the warm kitchen up the road with Edith reading me a bedtime story. But the empty dining room refused to go away.

It was here more than anywhere else in the coming weeks at St Mary's that I would always remember most vividly. Every night just before 6pm as the youngest child staying in the convent, supper would be served to me in this horrible echoing place, with the saints gazing down empty-eyed from the walls. Every night I must sit here in silence with no one to talk to and no one to help me forget.

The whole of life at the convent centred round the chapel as bells rang endlessly from the Angelus to Benediction. Silent scurrying nuns, heads bowed, arms folded, apparently without feet or hands, glided purposefully in and out of this peaceful little sanctuary at the top of the stairs.

When no one else was around I loved to go in there by myself. Up here we were level with the top branches of the old cedar trees where grey squirrels sometimes played in the shadows. Beside the altar a soft red lamp glowed permanently, telling me that our blessed Lord was actually "there" in the sacrament. It was strangely comforting to find myself alone with Him in this peaceful place.

Other things were more of a mystery, like the old nun who slept behind a curtain in my bedroom. Often her snores would keep me awake as I watched the moonlight through the cracks in those heavy shutters and wondered why it was that I wasn't even allowed to look at her in bed. Rumour had it that nuns were not even allowed to see their own bodies in the bath, washing their whole bodies secretly beneath great all enveloping shrouds tied right up to their necks. It seemed that for anyone to look at what lay beneath those heavy forbidding black robes would be the most terrible sin.

Mystery seemed to surround so many things. As the nuns prepared us for our first communion, I could only find myself worrying about exactly when the "blessed sacrament" became the body and blood of Jesus, and how on earth I was going to be able to get this down inside me. I remember feeling gingerly round the edges of the host with my tongue and struggling to understand this particular enigma.

There were only two other children living in this habitation of nuns, and being several years older than I was they had little time for the likes of me. As the days went by it felt as if everyone that I had ever known had abandoned me and gradually I suppose I began to withdraw into myself, no longer even wanting the company of others.

I still attended the Convent School next door, but I was not a part of their world any more. Without a welcoming home to return to and a place where I could belong it was as if I had become another quite different child. Often I would wander off by myself in search of solitude, and the other children now left me severely alone. Probably they felt I did not want to know them any more.

About this time I discovered the wonderful world of fantasy - a kaleidoscope land of colour and excitement, where one could wander at will among the corridors of the mind. It was to be a lifeline for me for many years to come, and still today if I catch myself unlocking the gates of that secret garden I know that I am trying to escape again.

Next door to the convent just over the wall were the old Cambridge Botanical Gardens - a world full of exotic trees and plants with little bridges leading over ponds and streams thick with water lilies and hoarsely croaking frogs. Lily pads and strange twisty branches were the

13

most perfect habitat for little creatures born of my imagination who, needless to say, lived in a world without problems and without pain.

It seemed like an eternity before I heard from my father again, although it is possible that only a few weeks had gone by.

One day on my return from school Sister Anthony met me coming through the gate into the convent garden and took me over to sit by the sundial. I remember that she took my hand in hers and then said that it was going to be very hard to have to tell me something.

The hospital had rung to say that my father would not live through the night and he was calling for me to go and say goodbye. I could scarcely bring myself to hear the words and everything in me wanted to run away from that time and that place - back into my sunlit fantasy world where there was no weeping and no sadness.

But this was reality and I would have to face it somehow.

"We must find him a little present for you to take," she said, but I could not think of anything except that he was leaving me. Eventually we settled on a beautiful blue clematis from the convent wall, and Sister took a little lead cross from the copious folds of her habit. She said it would help him to think of our Blessed Lord when he crossed over into the next life. I remember thinking that wherever that was then I wanted to go there too, because certainly there was nothing left for me to live for down here.
It was a long way to the hospital and when we eventually found my father he was propped up on his pillows in an enormously high bed looking white and exhausted. His face seemed waxen and almost transparent when I was lifted up to kiss him, and I was torn between a longing to cling to him and to run as far away from that place as I could possibly go. Already I knew that he was departing on another journey on which I could not join him.

Later that night when the nuns came to tell me that he had died they seemed shocked by my reaction. I could not even cry. A kind of frozen numbness seemed to have taken over and everything that went on around me seemed very far away as I withdrew within my own private walls of grief. Perhaps it was better so.

Chapter Two

All That Glitters

I sometimes wondered if I would be staying on at the Convent for ever. As each day went past it seemed I was becoming more and more of a permanent fixture in that dark silent building with its echoing bells.

When the loneliness was too much to bear I would creep in under the all-concealing branches of the old cedar tree and put my arms round its massive solid trunk, holding on as if my life depended on it. There was a timeless comfort in these shadows.

One wonderful day they told me that I was going to stay with my uncle and aunt near London and suddenly it seemed as if there might be hope for me after all. I had always adored my much older cousins, and it was such a relief to be part of a normal home again.

For several weeks I lived and played in their comfortable London home, attending the same school and gradually learning to unwind and to laugh again. It was safe here and I knew that they loved and wanted me. Or did they?

I have a very clear-cut memory of standing by the bay window at the front of the house waiting for cousin John to come home from school. On my left was one of those old mahogany wireless sets with thickly woven cloth between the arches of carved wood above the dials. I was actually standing in front of this at the time, so that its shape was burnt into my memory.

I imagine that I had said something to my uncle about how wonderful it was to really feel at home again. And even today I can still hear his voice echoing down the years, "Oh but you can't stay here Ann."

That was all - just one short sentence.

The sense of shock seemed to go right through me as I struggled to cope with this information. Where else could I go? This was the only other home that I had ever really known and where I felt completely safe. It seemed to me that I belonged here.

I have no memory of what happened next, but years later I was told that the neighbours had heard terrible cries as I was taken away.

Sometime after I had been returned to the Convent and my godmother, already in her seventies, had understandably pronounced herself unable to take on a seven year old child, a new and exciting happening filled my horizon.

A couple who I had never met were driving all the way up from Buckinghamshire to see me because they had always wanted a little girl of their own and were not able to have one.

My excitement knew no bounds and I could not restrain myself from listening outside just as the door had shut on Reverend Mother's study.

Minutes later the door burst open and I scarcely had time to run back to the safety of the staircase. Apparently it was obvious to all concerned that I had been listening!

As it happened, this action was to prove the decisive factor in my adoption. My new 'mother' had experienced strong doubts as to whether she could take on a seven year old child - a "jelly well set" as she was later heard to say - but my ill-disguised enthusiasm had apparently swept those doubts completely away for her.

My 'father' on the other hand had always wanted a little girl, and as he told me often, the acquiring of a small fair-haired seven year old seemed the best possible answer to his dreams.

The decision was made in just a few minutes and I was led in shyly to talk about my new life and my new home.

They bought out photos of what seemed to me the most idyllic place - an old country house that stretched out its welcoming arms to me, even from those few black and white photographs - a swimming pool completely circled by a beautiful rock garden, a great big orchard, and even a tennis court.

As they left that day promising to return once the adoption papers were signed and all the arrangements duly made, I could scarcely contain my impatience for the great day to come. This time my imagination was really working overtime, filling this new garden with lovely creatures from my fantasy world and housing all my toy animals in the hollows of that wonderful rockery.

As I later discovered, the adoption had been arranged by a friend of my godmother's, and since the transaction was a private one there was apparently little more than a cursory examination of the suitability of my new parents. In fact the whole process had to be rushed through the courts since it was shortly to become illegal to adopt someone of a different religion or denomination. And as I was soon to discover, my mother loathed Catholicism with a hatred born of years of prejudice. She did however promise with great reluctance to allow me to attend a Roman Catholic school.

Looking back from this distance I am sure that there were no wrong intentions on either side. My godmother saw only an enthusiastic couple with a really nice house, and they in turn took note of her title and the eminent suitability of this arrangement. The social worker was probably only called in as a technicality to tie up any loose ends. And thus the adoption was duly signed and sealed in the hallowed precincts of the House of Commons, since their mutual friend and sponsor was also a Member of Parliament.

Blissfully unaware of any of this, my excitement knew no bounds as my father's big grey car arrived to collect me from the Convent, carrying me away to my wonderful new home.

It seemed to me that my unhappiness had finally come to an end and I would be home in a place where I could really belong at last.

But alas, I have always been an incurable optimist, and if I had only known it the problems had scarcely begun.

When we eventually got to my new home I felt curiously diffident and unsure of what to do next. Whilst my father put the car away my mother rushed past me to let out the real love of her life - an enormous black and brown Airedale dog who leapt cavorting round and round her, whilst she lavished all her attention on this extraordinary creature.

"Don't be afraid of him, he won't hurt you," she called cheerfully in my direction.

I was not afraid of him, but once again a stab of that familiar rejection hit me from a direction where I had least expected it.

When my father returned he quickly called her attention to my existence and to the fact that I had no idea where to go and what to do. But as always it was he who took me up to the sanctuary of my little room up under the rafters, and then showed me where everything was around this lovely old house with its thick wooden beams.

As the days went by I found it incredibly difficult suddenly to "become" another person with even a different name. Time and again I would forget to call them mother or father, and they in turn would be deeply hurt, seeming not to understand how natural this was.

Another subject seemed to be absolutely out of bounds - and that was anything to do with my past existence. They had signed on for a new 'possession' who was apparently supposed to be a child fresh off the shelf with no memories and no past. Any mention of my own parents, the house where I had lived before, or even my life at the Convent was greeted with stony disinterested silence.

My father was even deeply hurt if I should ever mention to anyone that I was adopted - though to this day I have no idea how he thought people could fail to observe this fact! I am sure he meant it for the best of reasons, but it left me curiously bereft of my own past - as if a part of me had to be cut away for ever if I was to become 'acceptable' in my new home.

And so it was that the anticipation of my wonderful home grew into a slightly less than wonderful reality.

The garden was just as lovely as I had expected and seemed to stretch for miles. Right at the bottom and just beyond the boundary the countryside opened up into a wide circular area that had once been the site of an old Roman Camp. Around the perimeter of this age-old spot the remains of an excavated moat provided a perfect haunt for secret games and hideaways with other children in the neighbourhood - and on my own too whenever I needed to get away.

Another favourite hiding place was the old willow tree by the gate under whose overhanging fronds I could escape into my secret fantasy world beneath brilliant green tracery.

Inside the house everything was different and always uneasy, with a tension in the air that began to creep into my very bones making me constantly nervous and on edge.

My new 'mother' proved to be the most volatile of people, whose moods swung from one extreme to the other with total unpredictability. She seemed to positively flourish on rows and arguments, apparently forgetting completely what had been said only minutes later - whereas I would still be reeling from the blows for many hours afterwards.

On other occasions she would refuse to talk to me for hours on end if I wasn't behaving as she thought I should - although she would talk in perfectly normal pleasant tones if anyone else should come to the house.

To a small and rather insecure seven-year-old life with my new mother was often quite frankly terrifying, although as I discovered in later life she was blissfully unaware of this fact.

At one moment she would be ecstatically happy and I was expected to be her ever constant playmate, delighting in everything she said and did - and at these times she could certainly be great fun. But on other days there were terrible moods of black anger and despair, where she would scream and yell at me as if I had no right to exist.

Looking back from this distance I don't think she had ever really grown up, and it was significant that to the day she died her family still referred to her as 'baby'! Witty, charming and amusing when she wanted to be, it never seemed to occur to her that other people had needs. And many times it felt as if I was expected to be the parent in the relationship, even at this impossibly early age!

The dog was another constant source of trouble between us, and much as I love animals, life with my mother conditioned me to greatly resent the amount of attention people lavish on them. There never was the slightest doubt in my mind that if the house had caught fire she would first have rescued Ben and left my father and me to burn!

One of my regular duties was to "walk the dog" out on the Camp behind the house. Ben was a delightful creature, but as he stood almost level with my shoulders he was, to put it mildly, far too strong for a small child to control. Moreover, he had not the slightest idea of what the word obedience meant, charging off at will in the direction of a neighbour's hen house on the other side of the Camp.

Needless to say I got into terrible trouble whenever this happened for not having kept him properly 'to heel' - a total impossibility in my experience! So in the end I settled for keeping the wretched animal on the lead as soon as we were out of sight of the house.

This was fine until my mother began to suspect that poor little Ben wasn't getting his full ration of 'walkies', and lay in wait for me one day with a pair of field glasses trained at the ready. Blissfully unaware of this fact I was nicely caught out when I lied as usual when asked whether I had given Ben a proper walk!

As the days went by I learnt to stay out of my mother's way as much as possible and to cling to the shadow of my father whenever he was home. He was a big gentle man with a wonderful smile that seemed to split his face in two, and I grew to love him deeply.

Outside our home, as I was shortly to discover, he was very highly sought after as one of the greatest sound experts of his day. His name still graces the titles of countless old films, and he was well known and loved by actors and production staff alike. Many signed photographs and personal messages from almost every known film star of the time. And autographed books from people such as Baroness Orczy and H G Wells bear witness to how many people respected him.

More than anything I loved to go with my father to watch the films being made at Denham studios just down the road. Here I discovered a different kind of fantasy world created out of plasterboard, paint and pure illusion - but to a small child it was really magic.

I will never forget the Agincourt scene for Henry V, set in a misty blue night field with brightly lit tents strewn right across the studio floor. It was the first make-believe set that I had ever seen made up in real life. Or watching scenes filmed, apparently on the high seas in a howling gale, but actually right there on the studio set, with somebody rocking the springs on the 'boat' and a back projection of a real storm at sea being played on the screen behind the actors. And all the while my father was overseeing the orchestra playing suitable mood music exactly in harmony with action right there on the screen.

No expense was spared to make a picture in those days - a phenomena that of course increased as my father moved to the full glorious technicolour world of MGM at Elstree. Here the scenery seemed to change almost every week as the shape of the castle on the hill altered from Acre and the Crusades to the elaborate turrets of Medieval France, whilst the plasterboard houses in the valley no longer represented the jousting scenes of Ivanhoe, but had instead become an Indian village somewhere in the Wild West.

Sometimes there were over two hundred horses waiting in the stables, with so many armed extras ready to charge up the battlefield, whilst the furniture for period pieces were recreated in the studio workshops so as to be almost unmistakable from the genuine article even in real life. We still have some of the Tudor furniture left over from Henry the Eighth and a drum that belonged to Sabu the elephant boy.

There was a less than positive side to these experiences as I discovered if I ever watched a film with my father, he could not seem to help himself from letting out a compulsive groan whenever some actor he disapproved of appeared on the screen.

"Oh no, there's old so-and-so again - he really is the most dreadful ham."

And whilst I was suffering through the final tragic scene of "Red Shoes", he said, "Good heavens don't cry - after all its only tomato ketchup."

My mother scarcely ever came to the studios, and since she never entertained people in the house either it seemed that their worlds never met. As I soon discovered, she disapproved strongly of film people generally, never ceasing to tell me how synthetic and unpleasant they were in real life.

My father's policy was, as always, to ignore her outbursts of temper completely.

"Don't take any notice," he would say. "It's like water off a duck's back. Just let it roll off you."

Possibly he could do this, but for me these bitter angry outbursts usually went straight to the heart and stayed there.

For many months after my parents' death I had often woken in the night suffering from recurrent nightmares and sleepwalking, but if my mother ever caught me she would refuse to believe that this was genuine.

"You're a liar, a little liar," she would scream at me as I struggled to come out of a deep sleep and work out for myself exactly what I was doing out on the landing, or making my way downstairs.

Perhaps there was good reason for her anger as time went by. My father was coming home later and later these days, and whenever I heard his car pull into the driveway I knew that a violent argument was just about to break out. I would lie in bed for hours sometimes listening to their raised voices in the kitchen just below my room, feeling more and more afraid, more terrified of life in this unpredictable new 'home'.

In desperation one day I took the risk of telling my social worker when she called on her regular visit to enquire how things were going. As I was soon to discover, these questions were merely a formality for her, since she clearly found it hard to believe that anything could possibly be really wrong. Indeed, as the months went by I quickly realized that absolutely no one could see beyond the material facade that was "my wonderful new home".

Strange how appearances can so easily deceive even the most well-meaning of people! It was not long after this that my trust in human nature finally died an untimely death, and it was to be many years before I would ever risk telling anyone again just how bad things really were in the cellars of my life.

Chapter Three

The Death of Trust

It had been arranged that every summer I would go to stay with my godmother in her welcoming grey stone house on the wind-swept cliffs of Cromer. This year as I set off for the first time since my adoption, I left my new home with the most enormous sense of relief, secretly vowing that I would never again return to those bitter night rows and my mother's violent flaring temper. Surely, I reasoned, at least my godmother would take me away from that terrible place.

Aunt Avie's house with its grey stone walls and thick buttresses set against the North Sea gales seemed like a wonderful haven from all that had gone before. She was a delightful old lady and I can still see her wrinkled welcoming face in my mind's eye.

Here everything seemed at peace and normal again, as if one had returned to the world of sanity where smiling people came and went and life went on without fear or tension.

Every morning I would set out barefoot along the sands with her dogs trailing behind me as I had always done since I was a small child. Together we went in search of tiny crabs in the seaweed covered rock pools and then along the cliffs much further down the coast where stories of a sunken village that had fallen into the sea one dark and stormy night were legend - and where I always listened hopefully for the sound of the echoing church bell that was said to still toll beneath the waves.

As each new day went by and I began to relax and enjoy life again, I tried to get up the courage to tell my godmother about how terrifying I was finding life in my new home and how I dreaded going back there.

She had made no secret of her horror at my appearance when I arrived - at the shorn haircut my mother had forced upon me and at the handful of 'unsuitable clothes'. But a quick phone call to a friend had searched out some nice cottons from another family, despite the restraints of rationing, and after several weeks in the safety of my godmother's home I was beginning to feel human again.

One thing I knew for certain was that my godmother's new housekeeper did not want me in the house. Possibly the untidy presence of a small child was a threat to her immaculately tidy and ordered world, but the occasional remark would indicate to me all too clearly that she could not wait for me to leave.

All too quickly it was time for me to go and a letter from my mother had told Auntie Avie that she was longing to have me back. My heart sank further and further into the abyss, and still I could not bring myself to say what I was really feeling.

On the last night, and with the total lack of timing that young children so often achieve, I finally plucked up the courage to tell her. Newly washed and scrubbed and in my dressing gown ready for bed I knocked timidly on her study door. At the sight of her smiling welcoming face all the pent-up fears and feelings came tumbling out.

She was obviously visibly shaken at the full extent of my feelings - but still she kept struggling to try to understand. Are they unkind to you? What do they row about? What exactly is the trouble? Perhaps she could not cope with the fact that her judgement had been so badly wrong.

"Your father is such a charming man," she kept repeating, shaking her head in bewilderment.

At last it was decided that I should stay in the safety of her house for another few days whilst she looked into the problem. Definitely she would not send me back to them unless she was satisfied that I would be well cared for and happy.

I have no way of knowing what went on in the secret enclaves of those next few days, but in the meantime I lived in a fool's paradise convinced that from now on everything would be alright - just like the fairy tales. Only later in life did I realize how very few stories really have happy endings!

Finally, on the third night and just as I was really beginning to believe that all my troubles were finally over, I was told that my mother would be ringing me that evening during supper.

Earlier that day the housekeeper had made some pointed remark about, "How natural it was for a little girl to want to stay on by the seaside but that we all had to realize that holidays could not last forever."

Was that what they all believed?

As soon as I heard my mother's voice I knew she was in tears. What on earth was she going to do without her little playmate? How desperately she had missed me for the past few weeks. How she simply couldn't believe all the things I had been saying - after all, what were a few little arguments?

I knew that I was beaten and that there was nothing I could do now. She had appealed to my better nature and I could not refuse to help her. Echoes of another time when I had let my own mother down so badly were still too fresh in my mind.

Next morning when she arrived to collect me with a family friend in tow she was almost bristling with indignation. The story was more than a little different now. Full of righteous anger at my 'betrayal' she spent nearly the whole journey home telling her friend how 'dreadful' I had been and what 'lies' I had been telling to turn my godmother against them.

I slouched back in the corner of my seat in absolute silence. After all, what was there left to say? Childlike trust was rapidly turning into bitter cynicism and a complete lack of faith in anything good that people promised. It was a hard old world out there, and I reckoned I already had plenty of cause to know this firsthand!

At least my father seemed overjoyed to see me home again, though I was puzzled that he never said a word about all that had happened. Gradually I began to understand that this would always be his way - to take the line of least resistance, and to trust to luck that everything would turn out right in the end.

To my childish amazement the night-time rows seemed suddenly to have stopped! My mother's raised voice with yells and violent screams of outrage no longer wakened me from deep sleep in the middle of the night, and even the daily rows about little things round the house had dwindled to minor disagreements.

Suddenly it seemed that my mother was all sweetness and light, and I almost began to believe that I had been dreaming about all that had gone before.

Then one day when I was coming in from my dog walking duties, I found my mother seated motionless at the kitchen table with tears streaming down her face and a letter clutched in her shaking hand.

After that all hell was let loose and the rows reached a hitherto unknown crescendo.

It seemed that someone was citing my father as co-respondent in a divorce case and that for many months now he had been spending more and more time with another woman. In effect, as even I realized looking back, all those nights when he had officially been 'working late' and hence the terrible rows on his return.

My father made no attempt to deny the charges, and in fact he took the opportunity to announce that he was leaving anyway. He too wanted a divorce and would shortly be leaving to go and live near Elizabeth in California. That very night he slammed out of the house leaving me alone to my fate.

Divorce was almost unheard of in those days, and the very mention of the word was cause for the most terrible scandal. My mother effectively went to pieces and I could not help but feel sorry for her. She was almost chain-smoking now and her nicotine stained hands shook as she tried to cope with the most mundane tasks.

I had no idea what was going to happen with regard to my existence, and I heard nothing from my godmother or the social worker. Certainly it never occurred to me to ask if they knew - after all what was the point? It was already crystal clear that nobody cared.

The house was up for sale now with no shortage of would-be purchasers. My mother and her friends searched hard to find us somewhere to live, and eventually discovered a horrible dark little house half a mile from family and friends on the other side of the village. I loathed it on sight, and everything that happened there in subsequent years only underlined the despair that I had felt when I first saw the place.

My father never came home any more and I missed him terribly, but at least my mother's cronies acted as some kind of antidote to her black moods and sporadic attacks on me.

One day, shortly before we finally left Olde Tyles, she was very clearly on edge.

"Your father has asked if he can take you with him to California. 'That woman' has a big ranch there and apparently there is a pony waiting for you. He wants you to go and have lunch with him today so that you can meet her for yourself." Her voice trailed off into tears.

"You would have a much better life there," she hesitated trying to control herself. "I do realise that life hasn't been easy for you here." She blew her nose and rushed out of the room.

I felt quite guilty, but inevitably my hopes began to rise and I could scarcely wait for lunchtime to come. How wonderful it would be if things turned out for the best after all - but did I dare to hope this time?

All the way to the hotel my father was regaling me with stories of this wonderful woman who would love me and take me in, and how we would be such a happy threesome together. I heard endlessly about the ranch and our rosy future together, and he scarcely seemed to think of what all this was doing to my mother or to me. Although he did say once that he would make it all up to me somehow.

For once my mother was right and the 'other woman' turned out to be just as dreadful as she had said. With the frightening insight that young children often possess, one look at her told me just how plastic and insincere she really was. Everything about her made me cringe. What on earth did my father see in her?

After lunch, when she had oozed charm over me in the most sickening way, my father suggested that I should go out and watch the boats on the river whilst they had a little talk together. This was clearly going to be the moment of truth.

He seemed very quiet when I got back into the car to be driven home, and I waited for the news that I guessed was going to come. He was nervously fingering his tie and clearing his throat as he had a habit of doing when trying to think what to say.

27

"I'm afraid we're not going to be able to take you with us to America after all," he said. "Elizabeth is sure you would never settle there, and that it would be much kinder to leave you with your mother."

There was a long silence as he looked anxiously in my direction to see how I was taking this. "She does really need you now," he went on, turning the knife in the wound.

I think at that moment I began to experience what betrayal of trust really meant. In his own way I knew that my father loved me, but if it came to sacrificing anything that he really wanted, then clearly I was the one who would have to go without.

She had forced him to chose between us, and he would take the easy road open to him whatever hell might lie ahead for me - and he, more than anyone, had cause to know exactly what this would be like.

It was only a matter of months since they had lured me back from my godmother's house pretending that there was nothing at all wrong in their relationship that I could possibly have reason to complain about.

I was just nine years old and barely eighteen months earlier my father had signed the adoption papers promising, I imagine, to look after me for the rest of my childhood.

When I returned to Olde Tyles my mother could scarcely credit that I was going to stay on with her after all. For years afterwards she would ask me at regular intervals why I had made this choice. I had not the heart to tell her that the decision had been forced upon me, and in any case I would not have wanted to live in the same house as the woman I had just met!

Chapter Four

A White Blackbird

I would have to scour the caverns of my mind to think of anything good to say about the next few years of my life, for every moment is torn and stained with the deep purple of misery and wretchedness.

No sooner had my mother's friends helped us to settle into that horrible dark little house on the other side of the village than they disappeared off the scene completely. Probably even they had had enough of the terrible tears and temper tantrums that occurred almost daily now.

Whatever the reason the end result was the same. My mother effectively became my sole charge and my endless responsibility.

Most of the time it was as if our roles had been reversed and she would call to me pathetically, "Oh Ann, please help me," - which of course I was glad to do, but it was never enough.

When I returned home from school she was often still in bed with the dishes unwashed in the sink and the dog desperate to be taken out. Every day as I walked the last few yards hesitatingly up the road with my heart in my mouth, I had no idea what would be waiting for me.

One day she would be slumped in a darkened room unable to eat anything, and the next she would be waiting for me just inside the door ready to scream at me for some small misdemeanour. At one moment I was her greatly loved daughter and her only lifeline, and at the next a convenient whipping post for everything that had happened to us.

"Your father would never have left us if we had not adopted you."

"It's all because of you that I have to keep up this house."

And so it went on from day to day.

Looking back now I can feel genuine sympathy for the state in which my mother found herself. She had always led a very sheltered life and clearly found it very difficult to cope with problems at the best of times.

Moreover, since divorce was almost unheard of in those distant days, probably no one understood what she was going through or would have any idea how to help if they did.

But for me it was worse than anything I had hitherto experienced.

Memories around this time are pretty jumbled and chaotic, which I suppose is hardly surprising.

I remember travelling to school each day with the daughter of my mother's friends down the road, and then begging them to let me stay for tea afterwards rather than have to go home and face the music. If I was allowed to stay on there, this was the most wonderful oasis - at least for a couple of hours.

But then one day the ultimate disaster happened and this normal happy family moved away to buy a farm right up in Suffolk. For both of us their departure heralded the end of 'survival', and if things had been bad before they became a hundred times worse now.

In my mother's eyes their departure was the ultimate betrayal! They had 'no right' to leave her at a time like this or for that matter at any time. Looking back now I think they were her only real friends and it took her many years to forgive them. Years later she refused to even consider allowing me to be a bridesmaid at their daughter's wedding!

From my point of view their departure removed my last lifeline of sanity and normality.

The burdens became so great that even my schoolwork came to a grinding halt. I remember one Monday when the marks for the previous week were due to be read out, playing truant from school and just wandering aimlessly round the Common, with nowhere to go and no way out of the dilemma I was in. My mother had been in such a terrible mood for the whole of the previous week that it had been impossible to find anywhere or any peace of mind to even think about homework, and I had handed in nothing at all.

I imagine that after two or three weeks of this the school finally woke up to the fact that something was really badly wrong at home - one could say 'about time!', but then I suppose I had not been at that particular school very long. As soon as we moved away from Olde Tyles my mother had insisted that I must also leave the Convent Day School I had hitherto been attending.

However the terms of the adoption forced her to allow me to go for religious instruction to the old Catholic priest near my new school, and this would remain my one lifeline throughout those terrible years. I don't know how much I was ever able to tell him, but I was always aware of his caring presence and looking back I am sure that he would have been praying for me.

Now that the collapse of my schoolwork showed up the full extent of the crisis, things began to happen very quickly. Both my father and the social worker finally re-appeared on the scene in the same week, and lengthy conversations had obviously been going on with my godmother as well.

Looking back from this distance I find it hard to believe that no one had realized that anything was wrong before this time, but then perhaps they did not want to know. Where were my godmother, my uncle or even my social worker during those two terrible years. Is it possible they did not really know what was going on?

But I suppose if I am honest, I would probably never have told them just how bad things really were even if they had taken the trouble to ask.

After all, experience had already proved to me just how pointless appealing to people like this could be, and how counterproductive! At the end of the day, I was the one who would be shut in with my mother's outraged reactions and with what she would inevitably have seen as yet another 'betrayal'.

It had already been programmed into me that admitting to anyone that I had needs or that I hurt was a complete waste of time. Somehow I would just have to learn to cope with life and build a shell around my inner hurts that would protect me from all would-be invaders.

The final upshot of all these discussions and phone calls was the decision that I should now become a boarder rather than a day girl, and as soon as possible. My sense of relief was almost overwhelming - at long last I would be free from it all!

Of course no one told me that you carry yourself and your problems with you wherever you go, just like a tortoise carries its shell on its back - and that your life experiences cannot just be detached at will!

Although I did not realise this at the time, everything that had happened to me over the course of the past few years was rapidly turning me into a seriously insecure and unhappy little creature - something that I would never be able to 'change' by just getting away from home.

But my imagination was already working overtime and I was about to be transported to the exciting boarding school world of Enid Blyton's Chalet school or some such - which is probably about as far removed from real life in a girl's boarding school as one could ever hope to get!

My mother eventually deposited me in my appointed dormitory, with all that she herself thought 'necessary' from the great long clothes list sent to her - and went on her way tear-stained and troubled. To my shame I heaved an enormous sigh of relief.

To share a whole dormitory with nine other eleven year olds sounded the most enormous fun, but I quickly began to get the feeling that the rest of them were not nearly so enthusiastic about my arrival as I was about coming.

Looking back it is easy to see that nothing about me fitted into their comfortable uncomplicated middle class little world.

In the 21st century it is hard to believe, but I was in fact the only child in the entire school with divorced or separated parents. I was also the only Roman Catholic in a school that was fiercely Church of England and protestant to the core - thus evoking constant digs from the headmistress, who could really hardly tolerate my alien presence.

But worst of all for me was the fact that I possessed just **one** single ugly mufti dress (dark green with multi-coloured spots on it!) and just **one** faded brown check skirt and blue jumper - when at least **six** items of mufti were required on the school clothes list, and most children had much more than this!

To the other girls in the school this pathetic 'wardrobe' made me the ultimate laughing stock - and little girls are certainly not noted for their charitable tolerance of such matters!

Before many months had passed I was probably even more bitter about life than I had been before. I felt alienated from almost every recognizable group of girls in the school by virtue of how unwanted they made me feel, and the horrible clothes I was forced to wear. And as a final last insult, whenever other parents came flocking to be with their children for special occasions, school plays and matches, no one ever so much as crossed the threshold to visit me.

My mother could not possibly 'cope' with these occasions, or 'be seen without her husband' - and hence the fact that I had to be seen by all and sundry to have no one in the whole world who cared about me.

As the months went by I withdrew completely and finally into my shell. Most of the time I spent up in the library, devouring every available book, or down in the studio painting endless trees and sunsets.

And for the rest of the time there was my ever present fantasy world to walk out into at will. From the fairy tale creatures of my earlier years I had now progressed to living in a beautiful house by a sheltered sea cove, with my own sailing boat and a white horse on which to canter over the distant hills. In this private fantasy world I was well known and loved wherever I went, rescuing people in trouble and being highly sought after.

In real life I was probably busy turning into a little horror!

I hated their petty pointless little social world where stupid things mattered so much, and with all my heart I wanted to hurt them back.

For a while I had just hung around the school looking lonely and miserable, probably hoping that someone would take the trouble to ask me what was wrong - but of course they never did. Then finally one of the teachers who was obviously much shrewder than the rest took me on one side.

"Look Ann," she said, "I've got an idea that things are pretty bad for you, and you probably have very good reason to feel sorry for yourself, but acting like this is never going to do you any good. Just try and make the best of what you have got and see what you can achieve."

She had challenged me to make something of my life, and this proved to be the spur that I so badly needed. Slowly but surely I began to work my way out of the pit I had been stuck in, until by the end of that year I was top of the class in almost every subject. Needless to say this did not greatly endear me to my fellow classmates - especially as I was more than a year younger than everyone else - but secretly I took a great delight in their discomfort !

Suddenly 'achievement' had become an exciting new way to find acceptance, and it didn't stop in the classroom. I was pretty competitive on the games field as well, and then I discovered the possibilities of being 'noticed' through writing and acting as well. From the school magazine to skits in the house reviews. I soon discovered that I could keep myself in the limelight fairly continuously - they might not like me, but they certainly had to take notice of the fact that I was there!

Gradually but inexorably I was building the walls of success and apparent strength around myself that would prove so unassailable in years to come. It was a way of saying 'no one is ever going to get close to me again, because I am never going to allow them to see how much I hurt inside this façade'.

How many hundreds of times I have seen this syndrome working out amongst successful people in the world around me!

It would be nice to be able to say that something in the Christian influence of the school made a big difference to my life at this time, but it did not. If anything this aspect of life left me bewildered and confused as to who or what God really was, and what He expected of me.

Whilst I still attended the religious instruction with the old Monseigneur at the Catholic Church up the road, the headmistress left me in no doubt as to her acute suspicion about what happened at these times. More often than not she would haul me up to sit next to her at the high table the following night, and quiz me very obviously about what had been said and how long I had been 'alone with him'. Finally clamping down into a reluctant silence and taking no further interest in my wellbeing.

Up at the Catholic Church on the other hand I had found only loving acceptance. The housekeeper invariably made a special effort to cook me something nice for supper, and the old priest lovingly wended his way through the catechism with me, patiently listening to my questions and showing that he really cared about me.

He did however indicate that although school rules stipulated that I must attend their chapel daily, it was really 'not a consecrated church' or a suitable place to pray.

But then again, since I did have to attend school chapel every day, I actually came to love many of the old Anglican hymns and quite often to feel a sense of God's presence just as surely there as I did in the candlelit masses up at the 'one true church'!

So here I was suspended quite literally in mid-air between the two denominations, caught in a sort of religious tug of war that never ended.

At the time I did not even know that the last request of the Son of God on earth was the prayer 'that they (his followers) might be one' instead of the hundreds of differing warring denominations that now existed!

As a final last insult to the total unacceptability of my faith, when it became obvious to the headmistress that if I stayed on at the school she would have to make me head girl, my mother was asked to take me away.

"It would be absolutely out of the question to have a Roman Catholic in this important position," she explained.

Chapter Five

The Bridge

When I was about fifteen years old my father suddenly re-appeared on the scene. He had paid me very rare flying visits in the past few years whilst over from the States, but otherwise all I heard from him was the occasional letter on heavily embossed MGM lion headed notepaper - which I, as always, managed to wave around for everyone at school to see!

This time he told me he would be back in England for good.

Eventually I managed to extract the full truth from him about what had really happened. My mother had refused to give him a divorce, and Elisabeth had got fed up with waiting - and also with the fact that his money had now run out due to her Hollywood life style. He was flat broke and had nowhere left to go.

It was really wonderful to have him back and to get to know him again - although to begin with I must confess I found it hard to cope with the fact that he never even apologized for all the heartache his departure had caused me.

Shortly afterwards my mother announced that she had the most wonderful news.

"Quite by chance," she had, "just happened to bump into my father on the London train," and he had, "begged to be allowed to come home," saying, "what a dreadful mistake he had made and how much he had missed her." They were already making plans to buy a much nicer house just down the road, and "now we could all live together happily ever after!"

Just like the fairy tales I thought cynically to myself trying to look reasonably enthusiastic. Who did they think they were kidding?

I had lost all faith in my parents' 'promises' and 'good intentions'! It really seemed to me that I had carried just about all the problems and trials that it was fair to ask any child to bear and I had quite frankly had enough!

The only way to survive at home with my adoptive mother had been to concentrate fairly single-mindedly on her needs - and if this meant ignoring my own then so be it. After years of patient trial and error I had just about learnt to keep her on an even keel and to indulge her simple little wishes, to enthuse about her pampered animals, and thus avoid the worst ravages of her terrible temper.

For a start I knew that this state of affairs would be very quickly shipwrecked if my father came back to live with us - as indeed it was!

In place of a relatively quiet peaceful backwater we now returned to the appalling nail-biting tensions and rows of the days when I first went to live with them - and which my father as always allowed to run off him 'like water off a duck's back', whereas I could really hardly cope with this all over again - especially as they both now turned to me for support.

A new and even more unpleasant dimension was now added to the battle ground in which I quickly got involved right up to my neck.

Ever suspicious of anyone who might 'remove the love' of my father from her it was only a very short time before I also came directly into the line of fire.

"You could be your father's daughter you have so much in common!" she would storm at me as she found us discussing yet another intelligent subject that did not interest her rather childlike understanding. And as always I was caught in the crossfire, trying to defend the fact that I was spending time talking to my own 'father'.

The simple truth was that indeed I did have much more in common with him... he was an intelligent man and he also found her rather pointless, childlike view of life incredibly restricting - just as I had done all these years.

It was wonderful to have someone to talk to about all kinds of different things, and who really did seem to take an interest in me instead of just 'needing me'. But there was no way I wanted to get involved on this particular battle field! What was I supposed to do? Both of them insisted that I spend every waking moment with them - even trailing me off on holidays which we had never had before, and which caught in this particular parent trap proved, to be pure hell!

And then again both of them would regularly turn to me for help in coping with their marriage problems, as if I had some special insight which they lacked.

"Oh Ann, please help me - your mother doesn't understand."

In short I was back again in that familiar 'no win' situation, but this time caught in the role of the 'bridge' in their relationship.

As then finally, as the last straw, I was returned from boarding school at the headmistress's insistence awaiting my 'A' Level exams because I was too young to be allowed to sit these any earlier – and, of course, I could not possibly stay on to be head girl.

One holiday we went up to Scotland to see my father's family, and during the time there we paid a visit to St Andrews in order for him to play his traditional round of golf on the hallowed Royal and Ancient course.

One sight of this lovely old town and the university and I was hooked! From the old grey stone buildings and cobbled streets to the ruined cathedral on the cliff tops, and the picturesque Roman harbour this seemed to me the most wonderful place in which to spend three years studying. Oxford had originally been the plan, but St Andrews had one major advantage over any university in England - it was more than five hundred miles away from all the trials and tribulations of home life!!

And so it was that I found myself at King's Cross Station late one autumn evening waving goodbye to two tearful parents, and about to embark on a new life far away in the kingdom of Fife.

At long last I could honourably abandon them to work out their own problems, and leave all their fights and demands far behind me - and it was the most wonderful feeling of relief! From now on I vowed I would spend as little time at home as humanly possible.

Unlike boarding school St Andrews did indeed live up to the promise it had seemed to offer, giving me a completely new dimension to life. Suddenly all kinds of new possibilities opened up in front of me and I realized for the first time just how much I had been missing during those nightmare childhood years.

I gloried in the wide open spaces of Scotland, in the great expanse of seashore where I learnt to ride for the first time, and in the bluebell covered cliffs that rose steeply above the East Sands and the rock pools - where we would cook barbecues on long summer evenings, ferrying our boats and canoes across from the old Roman harbour. It was a whole new world and it was wonderfully exhilarating.

Another great blessing of university life was the freedom to mix and talk with so many people who thought and discussed the kind of things that really interested me. Suddenly I was no longer the odd one out, the only person who bothered to think about such things, but a normal and integral part of a world where I actually felt I belonged!

It seemed like a miracle. Was it really possible that this particular ugly ducking could have become a swan after all?

Although I would never have recognised this at the time, my adoption had rammed me like an extremely square peg into a very ill-fitting round hole indeed. And hence yet another reason why I never felt I 'belonged' or was 'acceptable'.

Chapter Six

First Love

In addition to all the wonderful things about life at St Andrews it was here for the first time that I fell in love. With his reddish hair falling disarmingly over one eyebrow Patrick towered over me. He was Irish and he clearly had not forgotten to kiss the Blarney Stone! His sense of humour and the appetite with which he approached life enchanted me - it was all just so much more fun when he was around.

We enjoyed all the same things from acting to messing about in boats and would spend many hours together caught up in lengthy discussions about the meaning of life. Throughout that long hot summer we were out scrambling along the cliffs above the East Sands, or walking up by the little stream that led down from Laed Braes to the old Roman harbour, and I will never forget the wonderful times we had together.

As exam time came round there was a sudden unaccustomed earnestness in the air and like most other students we lived on a diet of black coffee round the clock. I was not too worried myself as I knew we had the September re-sits to fall back on, but Patrick seemed to grow more and more tense as the exams drew closer.

Only now did I discover from his room-mate just how seriously his work had been going downhill. Moreover, since he was a second year student, if he failed the September re-sits this year he would certainly be sent down. Even then I still could not believe that this would ever happen - after all he was so intelligent, so alive.

That September as we met up outside the Examination Halls for the inevitable re-sits I finally realized with a sinking heart just how serious things were for him. And to my horror, when the examination results were published, Patrick had indeed failed just as he feared.

What on earth would he do now? I agonized, knowing he would never be satisfied with the ordinary kind of job that was all he would find without a degree behind him.

To my amazement he was back at St Andrews as if nothing had happened when the train pulled into the station for the autumn term. His father had paid for him to return to collect his things, but he had no intention of returning to Ireland for the foreseeable future - he was staying on there just to be with me, and he had already found digs across the square from my hall of residence.

I was delighted to see him, but something in me stirred uneasily. How on earth was he going to cope now that he was no longer a student?

Often on a Saturday we had got up at the crack of dawn to pick potatoes or muck spread out on a farm on the coast road just to supplement our meagre incomes. Now it seemed that Patrick was planning to earn his living doing this everyday - my heart sank.

I simply couldn't imagine him being contented with this kind of existence, and yet I did not want him to leave me either.

After just a few weeks of this soul destroying existence I began to notice the change in him.

His hands were red and rough and there was a feeling of hopelessness about him, as if he had finally realized just how much he'd thrown away.

I really did not know how to help him, or what to do for the best. Threatening letters from his father were arriving more and more regularly now, insisting that he return to Ireland and look to his own future. There was plenty of work available and he could not "play at farming forever".

Eventually Patrick yielded to this insistent pressure and very reluctantly packed up to leave. With a heavy heart I waved goodbye to him at the station whilst still believing he was doing the right thing.

As I walked away from the station, I knew I would miss him terribly, but the heaviness I had felt each day as I had watched him sink further and further into depression was almost more than I could bear.

I threw myself back into my work and into the world of drama and action. There were so many things to do and I had been deprived of a normal life for so long that I could not afford to hang around feeling sorry for myself.

We wrote to each other regularly, and although missing me, he sounded as if his life was beginning to come together. The end of the summer term was drawing closer and we talked enthusiastically of plans for me to join him in Ireland over the long vacation.

I was up to my eyes in a marvellous production of Macbeth in the old ruined castle on the cliff tops, where the waves lashed against the seashore and the atmosphere was exactly right.

Returning from my lectures one afternoon I was surprised to find a letter from Ireland awaiting me in a strange handwriting. Minutes later my whole world had fallen apart.

"He had taken his own life," his mother wrote, "with an overdose that must have killed him instantly." They had been away for the weekend and greatly blamed themselves for leaving him on his own - but they had absolutely no reason to suppose that he would ever do such a thing - or even that he was particularly depressed.

She enclosed a letter from him that he must have written just before he died and that she hoped "would not cause me too much pain."

In it he had written, "I love you but I cannot go on. Somehow I know that you will succeed and survive without me, but as for me I have thrown everything away and there is nothing left to live for."

My sense of guilt and failure was almost overwhelming. Did he really not know how much I needed him? Wasn't there something I could have done, even at this distance?

Suddenly I felt as if it was all my fault - as if I was somehow contaminated. With all the deaths and disasters that had followed me through my life, it seemed that I must somehow be a curse on all who came close to me.

Inevitably I collapsed with grief, retiring to the shelter of my darkened room completely unable to face up to life. The doctor came often to see that I was sufficiently sedated, and my room-mate did her best - but it was hopeless. I could not face the thought of life without him, and over and over again I blamed myself for not realizing how much he needed me. Exams were fast approaching but I could not even think about them.

The only reading that I could face was sad poetry and anything that tried to express the grief I felt.

But what on earth would happen to Patrick now? I had absorbed enough of the Catholic Church's teaching to know that suicide was seen as a "mortal sin" condemning one for eternity - but in no way could I bring myself to accept this. Surely there must be some mistake?

In search of some glimmer of hope I struggled round to the Catholic priest, but any hope of comfort from this source was quickly trampled under foot. "Suicide was the ultimate never to be forgiven sin" and at that time the "guilty ones" were not even allowed a Christian burial. As I left the church that day I vowed never to go back - for if this was what God was like then certainly I did not want to know him!

A terrible heaviness now descended on me, blocking out any small ray of hope that struggled through the blackout of despair. What was it about me that prevented me ever finding true happiness? Would nothing ever go right in my life? It really began to feel as if I had been personally destined for trouble from the day I was born.

Chapter Seven

Escape at Last

As the time came for me to leave university I was determined about one thing - that whatever happened I was not returning home to my parents' war zone!

My mother's attitude to Patrick's death had been almost the last straw in our relationship.

"Don't think you can play the tragedy queen here," she said tersely, promptly loading me with some other minor problem of her own.

I am sure that like so many of her generation she really had no idea of how to help me through the grief that I was feeling, but it certainly didn't make me any more loving towards her. And of course yet again my grief had to go underground.

I had applied for a job with the British Council in Finland and even before I graduated I was already on the high seas destined for the snowy wastes of the North and a little town called Kajaani.

We were barely two hundred miles from the Arctic Circle and throughout the winter months the sun scarcely came above the horizon, leaving us much of the time in perpetual twilight. It seemed an appropriate place to escape to and a hiding place where I could be alone with my sorrows.

Life was often as hard as the frozen lakes that surrounded us on all sides, and the people turned out to be almost as unassailable. So shy that one almost had to come at them with a pick axe to get them to open up at all!

Unfortunately, since a large part of my job consisted of giving English Conversation lessons I just had to try - but it was really heavy going!

I was the only English person in the whole town and I soon began to understand how crucial language and communication could really be. My landlady and I conversed in rather rusty German, and apart from that

I relied very heavily on one other family who had lived in the States for a short time and were reasonably fluent.

But in a curious sort of way I really didn't mind too much about any of this. For the first time in years I could be alone and try to work out for myself what life was really about.

There was no one to pressure me into doing or being something that I was not and gradually I think I began to unwind.

Most of my work had to be done in the evenings, so that throughout the day I was free to wander at will amongst the forests and the lakes and to drink in the pure uncluttered beauty of nature around me.

By Christmas time everything was covered in a thick blanket of snow several feet deep, and a great silence had descended on the town. Cars travelled with chains on their tires, biting into the soft white roads, and sleighs with their bells jangling echoed daily through the streets. The temperature was permanently many degrees below zero and frostbite was a very real danger. My landlady got very agitated if I ever attempted to open my bedroom window.

"Your brains will freeze," she informed me in dire German undertones!

By January the snow was ready for skiing and I took my first few timorous steps with what seemed to be the whole town watching me and screaming with laughter because I didn't automatically know how to do it! They had never met anyone before who could not ski almost before they could walk and any request to teach me met with incredulous laughter.

"Teach you! - well for goodness sake you just ski, it's that simple!"

They were only langlauf skis - thin whippy blades attached to your feet at the toes, allowing the heels to move at will travelling at high speeds over the frozen lakes and open hillsides.

Despite their lack of help I soon learned to get along somehow, spending almost every day out in the forests skiing along the multitude of beautiful valley tracks through bare silver birch trees etched out in ice and snow, and over gentle rolling hills and out across the solid ice covered lakes.

The incredible snow-laden landscape where the pine trees almost seemed to groan under the weight after a fresh fall of snow left me full of wonder at their beauty. Sometimes huge icicles blazed brilliant blue white and spiky from an overhanging branch and the air was sharp and cold against my skin. Often it seemed like an enchanted world from another planet.

The silence was everywhere with tiny tracks of the Arctic hare disappearing into the trees, and only the faint cries of the snowbird wheeling overhead. The beauty was endless, amazing, eternal.

Deep down I wanted to cry out against God and against all that life had done to me thus far - and yet how could I do this surrounded by so much in nature that was truly wonderful?

One great advantage of this remote corner of Finland was that there was no Catholic Church for miles, and no one to knock on the door and ask me why I was not coming to Mass. I had finally escaped the long arm of the Vatican.

In fact I had almost no contact with any kind of church life for the whole time that I was out there, and this took the pressure off me too, allowing me to think through what, if anything, I really believed.

Somebody was "there" - that much I knew from my earliest days alone in the Convent. But what was He really like, and how could He allow such suffering in a world that He was supposed to be running?

Looking back now I can see that He appeared to me rather like those who had "looked after me" up to this point in time - loving me if it suited him, but far away when he was most needed.

People often see God in the shape and nature of their own fathers, and as a result I could not bring myself to believe that He would ever be "there" for me when I really needed him, or that he would not just walk away when I was in trouble, after all this was what my own father had done often enough.

"Just like a father pitieth his children ..." say the psalms. Well if he was like my adoptive father there really wasn't much hope for me!

So that when I thought of God it was more in terms of judgement such as why I hadn't been to mass or confession recently! Any concept of Him 'loving' me was completely out - after all I scarcely knew what that meant. Thus far God seemed to have made sure that any love I experienced would subsequently be removed from me at the earliest opportunity!

If anyone had said to me, "All things work together for good to those who love God and are called by His name," I would just have laughed in their faces!

As the midnight sun came into its full glory, with the birds singing right through the night and an electricity in the air that made it impossible to sleep, I realized that I would soon have to return to England. I had signed a contract with the BBC before I left the country and I was due back there in June.

Part of me wanted to stay on there for ever, safely wrapped in a cocoon woven by nature. Swimming in the forest lakes at night after a wonderful sauna in a friend's log cabin, gazing up at the brilliant tracery of the silver birch trees in the full glory of their Spring green, and caught up in the little world of a tiny forestry town that had finally taken me to its heart and allowed me to belong. Perhaps if I had not signed that contract I might be there still.

As I set sail for the return journey after many tearful farewells, I knew that I would have to face up to harsh reality again before we actually landed.

For one thing I had decided never to go back to the Roman Catholic Church. And since I could not just walk away from God, I made up my mind to join the ranks of what I considered to be a perfectly 'safe' and undemanding denomination. In other words I would become C of E like everyone else! The sort of thing you could write on a form without any great stir - it was just normal and acceptable and this was all I wanted!

My parents were overjoyed by this decision, as if I had finally seen the light! I could never remember them going to church before this moment in time, but suddenly this seemed to be something that they wanted to do - together!! Strange that something like this should actually unite them after all these years.

We finally settled on a little church in the village of Fulmer where we all felt at home and told the vicar of my decision. Probably he was cannier than I gave him credit for, because immediately he asked me to go and see him for a few weeks first just to make sure I really knew what I was doing. He did not give me much choice, and so I reluctantly went along with this.

I think he was trying to point out that signing on to be "Church of England" wasn't just like joining a club, but that there was no real point to such an exercise unless this "membership" involved a personal relationship with God.

For my part I couldn't see why he bothered with all this - surely he must realise that I KNEW all about God - after all I had been attending "religious instruction" ever since I could remember! We agreed that the Catholic Church was wrong about certain things, that the Pope was certainly not infallible, and that it wasn't necessary for a priest to personally forgive every sin I had ever committed - but beyond that I just wanted a different label to my faith, and surely that was reasonable enough?

I listened politely, agreeing with everything he said, but not taking a great deal in. After all I knew what I was doing, and so far as I could see that was all that mattered. Finally, he was satisfied that he had told me enough to be going on with and then agreed to go through with the necessary service - it all seemed a bit elaborate and unnecessary, but eventually it was over and I could relax.

At last it was "official" - I was now Church of England and no threat to anyone. I had escaped and the Catholic Church had never even woken up to that fact, or got round to excommunicating me as they normally have done.

Chapter Eight

Media World

I was captivated by the world of the BBC from the moment I first entered the heavy bronze doors of Broadcasting House. In small anonymous studios an extraordinary variety of programs were being stitched together with just a handful of actors and tape sequences, records and sound effects.

We were given barely six weeks training in which to discover how to edit tape, make announcements, and cope with live transmissions on the air - what to do if the line from Belfast didn't come up as expected, how to cope with playing up to forty different discs in one program, coming in on exactly the right note, and all the usual sound effects such as rustling tape for autumn leaves, splashing around in bowls of water, or even firing a gun in the furthest possible corner of the studio.

But after that they dropped you in at the deep end! Their policy seemed to be that once you had made a mistake in front of an audience of several million this was unlikely to happen again - the policy definitely worked!

Of course a lot of the work was fairly mundane stuff, especially in the beginning. Pressing the green light for some nervous speaker to make his sound debut, playing the signature tune for Desert Island Discs, clapping together coconut shells for horses' hooves in a simple Listen With Mother story, or opening and shutting doors for Mrs Dale's Diary could hardly be included in the category of inspiration! But it remained a fascinating world that you left as you stepped back into the busy Regent Street traffic at the top of Portland Place after a day's work.

Often we had to do night duty, putting the late night programs on the air, and then collapsing into an uneasy sleep before getting up before dawn to rehearse the Today program - and incidentally making just as many mistakes as the presenter of the day! There was just something about these terrible early morning programs that seemed to make blunders almost inevitable.

In the few short hours of sleep that was all we would ever get, one would be tossing and turning and endlessly checking the clock since oversleeping would mean that some program would just not go out on the air and, even worse, that many thousands of people would know all about it!

Some of the worst programs were the overseas transmissions that went out all round the clock to different corners of the world from Bush House. On one occasion I managed to play a disc at double speed in the middle of the night without even noticing, until I wondered why on earth it had finished so early. And another time as I was sending out a dawn English by Radio program I forgot to shut the microphone fader before starting the disc. Wondering what on earth had happened since there seemed to be no sound coming from the disc, I was obviously muttering away to myself until I noticed the engineer's red light flashing.

"I suppose you are aware that all these colourful comments are being transmitted all the way to Latin America along with your English by Radio program," he commented cynically!

You knew you had "arrived" when producers started asking for you by name on all the best record shows. Somehow you had actually succeeded in getting exactly the right cross fades in a show with upwards of forty discs coming in on exactly the right note in mid record - apparently with effortless ease but in reality nail biting tension! Even now the sight of a red transmission light can still bring me out in a cold sweat!

There were plenty of crises of a different kind as well. Sight reading had never been a particular skill of mine, and it was always a struggle to laboriously follow each note on a musical score. I will never forget the blind panic of being left in charge of a whole orchestral transmission in the Albert Hall studio and leafing desperately through the score to see when the crescendos would come. A sudden burst from the brass section could still take the transmitters off the air in those early days, and you were supposed to take the faders down gradually beforehand so that the needle didn't swing over too violently!

I loved the audience variety shows as well - especially when they involved any of the Goon Show characters. They always took unholy delight in making up the script as they went along, completely confusing you over what sound effects you were supposed to be making next.

Sometimes we were positively aching with laughter by the time the program was over.

Another corner of my life was beginning to open up during this period. Whilst attending the local village church with my parents I met up with a girl who invited me to join her in a strange sounding thing called a 'Bible Study Group' in London.

Although this sounded rather daunting and a bit too serious for me, I really liked her and it seemed to me that this might provide a way out of the rather claustrophobic atmosphere I now found myself in living at home.

To my amazement this group consisted of perfectly normal people who were in fact great fun to be with. In addition to discussing what was in the bible (and which incidentally I knew almost nothing about!) we often had meals and weekends away together and did ordinary interesting things.

Gradually I began to see them as the kind of people whose values I could really respect, and who I actually wanted to be with. But it was curious - they talked about God as if He were an actual person around the place, so much so that on occasions if I turned round I almost expected to see Him there!

There was nothing long faced or artificial about any of these people and I soon became aware that almost all of them knew a great deal more about God than I did - although I would certainly never have admitted this at the time!

About this time the BBC sent me on a special course at their training centre near Evesham down in the Avon Valley. This meant that I was away from home for quite long periods of time - and away from my London friends as well.

There were none of my usual work mates on the course and we were thrown together at fairly close quarters with a number of other BBC folk from around the country, spending all hours of the day with them.

Since Patrick's death I had never allowed another man to get really close to me, although various boy friends had come and gone during this period. The pain and heart break that I had gone through in the months after he died, had seen to it that no one had been allowed into the inner sanctum of my feelings for a very long time.

Gradually as the weeks of the course went past one particular man seemed to be spending more and more time with me, and I had to admit that I really liked him. To begin with there was nothing serious about the relationship and in any case a sort of holiday atmosphere prevailed, since on a short course like this we were like ships that passed in the night.

It was only towards the end of the course that I discovered to my horror that he was already married - "unhappily" of course - as they always are! But unfortunately during this time away from home he had somehow managed to get through my defences and I was more attracted to him than I should have been.

However I told myself firmly, it was only for those few weeks and as soon as we both left to go our separate ways then obviously we would never see each other again.

Unfortunately it didn't work out that way at all. Because of his work it was child's play for Stephen to turn up outside the studio I was in or be waiting by my car in the parking lot, and this time I couldn't just get away as I had planned. Moreover, I really did like him and being with him fulfilled a need in me that I had not faced up to for a very long time.

There was nothing physical in our relationship about which I had cause to feel ashamed, but there was no doubt that the attraction was "there" - and by continuing to see him I was allowing the relationship to go on.

By this time I was fairly sick with myself. For years I had paid the price for my adoptive father's affairs with other women, and I had really despised him for the harm that he had done. And yet here I was doing exactly the same to someone else's wife - however "unhappily married" he really was.

Before I went to Evesham I had begun to feel myself getting closer and closer to a relationship with God, but now He could have been a million miles away. And I knew in my heart of hearts that this was my fault - that God would not come close to me when I was deliberately disobeying him

54

like this. And yet, I reasoned, hadn't I deserved a bit of happiness after all the bad things that had happened to me?

It never once occurred to me to ask God for help - this was simply not within my experience. A lifetime of being let down had taught me that God only helps those who help themselves!

And so I did what I had always done - run as far away as possible from the situation. It was very easy to get transferred round the country within the BBC world, and I quickly got myself posted to Glasgow, as just about as far as I could possibly get. In amongst the endless programs of Scottish dancing and bagpipe concerts, not to mention Gaelic plays that no one could understand, perhaps I would be able to escape?

But of course there was always the telephone, and after three months he was still there waiting for me when I got back.

The next time I tried Bristol and the world of the Natural History unit where people like Johnny Morris flourished and Gerard Durrell's iguanas got lost on the studio floor and mixed up with all the television cables.

But deep down I was beginning to realise that I couldn't possibly do anything about this situation for myself and that I really needed help. In fact Stephen was already laughing at me for even trying.

"Don't fight it," he said. "We were made for each other. You'll never get away from me, and you'll have to face up to this sooner or later."

One day in desperation I wandered into the church of St Mary Redcliffe. I can't remember much about the service, or even the exact content of the sermon, but the kernel of the message reached out to me with a clear gleam of hope in the darkness.

"Jesus had already paid the price for all our failures on the cross - and all we had to do was reach out and ask him for help and forgiveness." No trying harder, or doing better next time, or even so many days in purgatory!

And what was more He would help us in our weakness, strengthening us to cope with problems and resist temptation - because by ourselves we could do nothing."

Well I could certainly agree with that statement now, although a year ago I would probably have said that this was really pathetic and unnecessary - after all surely it was just a matter of will power!

That night I turned to God more in desperation than anything.

"If you are really there," I said, "and if it's true that you can help me, then please come into my life and do something about this mess that I am in."

No flashing lights or ringing bells, but just a sudden sense of peace and a quiet assurance that all would be well. I still don't know if I really believed this, but I had taken the risk of putting my trust in Him and now he would have to show me whether it was true or not.

I was due to return to Broadcasting House at the end of that week and of course this would be the acid test. And sure enough first thing Monday morning the phone rang.

"I need to see you tonight."

"It's over Stephen," I heard myself say very deliberately.

An incredulous chuckle came over the receiver.

"Oh yes! Sure, I believe you - so what is different this time? Don't tell me you have found someone else. At least you could have the decency to tell me face to face what has happened."

I did meet up with him, but the same inner strength and resolve stayed with me - a feeling of peace and of someone else gently taking over the reins of my life that I had never known before. Nothing outside had changed in the slightest - Stephen was still very much around, and still very determined, but something inside of me had changed very dramatically and I was astonished at the strength He had given me out of the blue.

When I told him that there was no one else, but that God had shown me it was wrong to go on with this relationship, he positively laughed in my face.

"God! You have got to be joking! What on earth does He have to do with it? All right have it your own way, but you'll be back. I know you will."

Before long he would discover how wrong he was!

Chapter Nine

A New Beginning

Life around me suddenly began to take on a new and exciting quality. In addition to a whole new group of friends that I really valued and who genuinely cared about me, new opportunities began to open up at work as well.

For some time now I had been trying my hand at writing different programs - talks for Woman's Hour, plays for Schools radio and so on. Now suddenly as these were actually broadcast, I was offered a new job as Scriptwriter in the Overseas Service at Bush House, and this proved to be a new and exciting challenge.

First thing each morning, every journalist in the department was given some news item to cover which would have to be researched and written up ready for transmission on all services that very same night.

Hitherto my writing had always been rather haphazard, depending very much on whether or not I felt inspired - but now I had no choice in the matter - and these few months experience would stand me in very good stead in later life!

The scripts had to be almost exactly five hundred words to fit into the required time slots and be available to go out in English or in translation on all of the forty two different language programs that went out round the world every day. All this from the hundreds of tiny studios that made up the incredible rabbit warren that was Bush House in those days.

There seemed to be no limit to the variety of subjects that we were expected to cover - a press conference with the Duke of Edinburgh about his new Award Scheme, a personal interview with Isigonis about the design the revolutionary new Mini that had only just come on the market, a new exhibit at the British Museum, or the first night of a play or film.

Sometimes I would start the day knowing nothing whatsoever about the subject that I was expected to cover, and frantically ringing round different friends to at least give me the necessary background information, or scouring the very comprehensive BBC library. This way at least I wouldn't have to admit to total ignorance on the subject during the ensuing interview! But once again this would prove to be very useful experience in later life, teaching me that you can actually find out about almost anything if you really make the effort and know who to ask.

Around this time I was invited to join a new study group in London, which was led by a rather good looking dark haired chap who I admired greatly from a distance. However, he seemed somewhat aloof and distant whenever I was around and I had the distinct feeling that he disapproved of me. In fact it turned out later that he actually thought I was impossibly "arty and unconventional" when he first met me!

I could not have been more astonished than when he first asked me out and I remember driving home that day wondering if I might finally have met another man to love after all. That was if I could actually take the risk.

As we spent our first few evenings of that lovely English Spring together I quickly realized how loving and caring Peter was and how much we had in common. But alas many and various problems lay up ahead for us in this relationship.

Before we got to know one another Peter had signed up to go and work for the family company in India, and he had been told that there was no way that we could possibly get married for the foreseeable future. In fact the contract actually specified three years, and his father was adamant that no son of his should be allowed exemption from Company rules.

Somehow it all seemed so much more than I could possibly bear - almost like a replay of the events before Patrick's death, and I was finding it really impossible to trust God with the future. What reason did I have to suppose that things would work out any better this time than they had done in the past?

Peter did his level best to help me with this, and very tentatively I stepped out to trust that God would see us through this difficult time. But perhaps I knew even better than he did that we would have a long hard journey ahead of us.

We spent the last few precious weeks of our whirlwind engagement on an emotional high that was accentuated both by his imminent departure and by the fact that I was terrified that something terrible would happen to him when he had gone - as I had already so traumatically experienced.

I shall never forget the tearful quayside farewell so soon after our engagement, as Peter departed waving into the blue. It really felt as if my heart would break, the road ahead seemed so impossible.

Indeed, hardly had he landed in India than it seemed as if my worst fears had been realized. Peter's plane into Assam was the last flight in before the Chinese invaded, and after this there was no further contact with the outside world - not even through the hot wires of the BBC news department where I hovered anxiously during the next few days.

The situation in Assam did finally resolve itself, since the Chinese overran their supply lines and withdrew back to the border. And eventually Peter and I settled down to a seemingly interminable period of writing each other long emotional letters just longing to be together again.

During this time my job was keeping me fully occupied, since I was now part of the time-honoured Children's Hour production team together with Uncle David, Larry the Lamb and a number of other old favourites. Here I was assigned to thinking up ideas for new series, and generally helping to write and produce the wide variety of programs that went out on the air every day.

However, Peter was completely on his own out in India, and the time was far worse than he could ever have imagined. The India he had heard such wonderful stories about had turned out to be a fairly lonely hostile place, away from everything and everyone he loved. Throughout this time he had been without any kind of fellowship and the enthusiastic vibrant faith he had once had seemed to have dwindled in the light of his loneliness.

Finally, a whole seven months later he managed to get permission to fly home during his 'local' leave so that at long last the wedding could take place. At last we would be together again!

We were married in the fresh green of an early Spring, and the contented glow of dreams at last fulfilled - though it would have been nice to have a moment to catch my breath and to have more time to recollect what my husband-to-be looked like before we met up on the altar steps!

Since he only had a fortnight's leave in total we left immediately after the reception for our honeymoon on the way back to India, and to the kind of married life I could not possibly have begun to imagine! It would not have taken a genius to predict that many and various problems lay ahead of us!

For years I had lived amongst film sets of strange faraway places and exotic locations but these had always disappeared once the scaffolding that propped up these make-believe worlds came into view.

As we drove away from Calcutta International Airport towards my first sight of a world beyond the sights and sounds of Europe, I found it hard to believe that all this could possibly be real. Surely these terrible scenes unfolding before me could only belong to some horror movie whose waking nightmare would terminate as always once we reached the edge of the set.

The hideous stench of poverty and despair that stretched for miles through shanty towns and slums seemed more impossible, more unreal than any film set had ever done. How on earth could people live out their starving ragged lives with so little hope?

Tiny emaciated children played with old tin cans in the gutter, dignified ragged women picked their way through enormous piles of festering rubbish by the roadside, and 'sacred' cows seemed to scavenge everywhere at will. People squatted as unconcerned as dogs to perform their bodily functions in full view of passers by.

Nothing that I had been told could ever have begun to prepare me for this world where families lived out their whole lives beneath ragged awnings on street corners, and lay sick or dying in the heat of the sun.

Occasionally a small fragment of bright green creeper struggling sparsely between tenement buildings, or a tattered yellow sari hanging out of a window to dry would momentarily light up the squalor, but the hopelessness hung all around me like a leaden weight. Almost impossible to bear.

Not long after this the new Dum Dum highway would bypass these terrible scenes, sparing arriving passengers the full horror of Calcutta's slum world, but the nightmare of those first few hours will stay with me always.

"It could not possibly be like that - no one would allow it!" I had protested to Peter as he had tried in vain to prepare me in his letters for what lay ahead. With the sublime arrogance of Western youth I had really imagined that I knew it all!

Throughout our years in India I struggled to try and understand. How could wealthy people not even lift a hand to help? Why did no one do anything? Where were all the caring people to come alongside and bind up the suffering and the brokenhearted? But all I ever heard from our Indian friends was the same despairing phrase, "What to do? It is will of God."

I actually found the lack of caring almost the hardest thing to bear and for the first time I began to understand the benefits of coming from a country based on Christian values - even if we did not always live them out.

The old man starving in the gutter was only there because of sins committed in his past life. Somehow he must struggle through the years without complaining, and above all without hope in order to atone for these - and maybe to be reincarnated to some better form of life next time round.

Mercifully we were to spend the first few years of our time in India in the green and pleasant safety of the Tea Gardens of Assam, where there was very little visible poverty and most companies operated a sort of mini welfare state where employees were housed and fed with schools and hospitals provided, and where the land produced a wealth of food for local farmers.

Chapter Ten

Tropical Home

Our first home turned out to be an old wooden bungalow set up on stilts in the middle of a tea plantation, with no other house in sight. The soft green flat 'table' of tea bushes stretched for miles into the distance, spaced only by occasional overhanging shade trees. From time to time a group of brightly coloured tea pickers would hover past, flicking the tips off the bushes with lightening speed, and passing on to fresh pastures. But our nearest neighbours were over half a mile away.

The heat during the monsoon when we arrived was almost unimaginable. The walls of our bungalow under the lights at night looked like moving wallpaper they were so thick with assorted and incredibly shaped insects, from enormous velvet moths and praying mantis to sinister horned beetles. Snakes, rats and cockroaches were so commonplace as to be hardly worth the mention!

No friends down the road; no possibility of working; no town anywhere in the vicinity, and few if any interesting activities to keep me occupied. In addition, there was this positively alarming fleet of servants who regularly turned up unannounced at the most unexpected moments - such as the bearer who used to make his way in from the back veranda straight through the bathroom, solemnly bowing to whoever happened to be sitting on the loo at the time!

The Company provided fourteen servants for all managerial staff, and it seemed impossible to get away from this veritable army! The caste system saw to it that not one of them would lift a finger to do a job that was beneath him, so that the cook would not even demean himself by washing his own saucepans! As we left one clearing up the breakfast things, sure enough another would be making the beds, and yet another beavering away in the kitchen.

We soon discovered that any hope of privacy in our newly married life was to remain an impossible dream! Besides which, since there was always some disagreement raging between them and few of them trusted the others, it naturally fell to my lot to keep the peace and somehow get things done.

65

During those seven long months apart we had written a great deal to one another - long searching letters about a great many things. On paper we communicated extremely well, but in real life this was not so easy.

Few Englishmen find verbal communication about this sort of thing easy and Peter was no exception. When I desperately needed to talk to him about my needs and feelings and to explore his own this territory proved to be totally out of bounds. "Feelings were unreliable," he insisted, "only actions and facts were important."

Having so suddenly been dropped onto a hot and humid plain in the North East of India a million miles away from the busy London life that I had lived in the BBC, I had plenty of needs and feelings that I was desperate to talk about... but unfortunately at the time I lacked the inner strength to insist that we did so.

On the few occasions that I tried he would simply become angry and defensive as if this was some kind of criticism of him - and so in the end I just gave up. In some curious way that I could not have explained this seemed uncomfortably like life with my adoptive mother all over again - as if I must deny my own needs altogether just as I had always had to do in the past. I really could not believe that this was happening in our own marriage.

It seemed to me that I had barely opened the door of my feelings before Peter had slammed this shut again right in my face. But whereas of course most other people in my situation would have persisted, I had as always given up almost immediately without even a struggle. Yet again it seemed there was no one in the whole world who really cared what I was feeling.

"Never mind," I told myself firmly. "Just keep quiet and get on with living as best you can." Peace, peace, peace at any price - the worst piece of advice you can possibly give anyone!

Inevitably with our very rushed engagement before Peter's departure for India, we had never given ourselves time to talk through our expectations of marriage - if indeed we had even thought about this in those terms!

Like so many people, we had both assumed that because we loved each other we would both fall over backwards to meet one another's unspoken expectations, and then of course we both felt hurt because neither of us knew what these actually were!

In my case coming from a broken home I had very little idea of how a marriage should work in practice - or how to make a success of this. And on the other hand I had plenty of experience of the "how not to's"!

Furthermore, I honestly do not think I had any idea of how much input and sense of self-worth my work had actually given me. And now that this had been taken away from me and there were no really supportive friends around either, every ounce of my self-worth seemed to depend on the ability of the man I had married to make me feel loved and wanted - and I guess that was a pretty heavy burden for anyone to carry, especially when Peter really had very little idea of how to go about this.

I am sure that if I had been a more secure person to start with - if I had not experienced such a divided childhood home - then I would have known what to do and been much more able to cope with the situation.

I will never forget the terrible emptiness of being left that first morning when Peter went off to work, with nothing but a rather ancient record player to fill the aching void! Peter was up to his eyes working eighteen hours a day at the height of the tea production season, and I was alone in a strange country scarcely even knowing who my neighbours were.

As I struggled to find some sense of self-worth and to put pen to paper reaching out to distant friends, I really began to wonder how I would survive. So many thousands of miles from home and from anyone that I could trust to talk to, the fears and failures continued to haunt me as I cried my heart out alone on the veranda in the cool of the night. Peter slept soundly and he seemed to accept my final silence as acceptance of the status quo.

I really did not know what to do. For years I had watched my parents mess up their own marriage and yet somehow blithely assumed that I would 'know' how to do better without any help on how to go about this. Was I being unreasonable to expect anything better of our relationship as Peter now implied?

After all the hurts and fears of my childhood, I could scarcely believe that this was happening all over again.

One thing I did very quickly understand was the reason for Peter's dwindling faith. There WAS no church in the area, though roughly once a month the 'padre' would turn up at the local Country Club to take a special service. On these occasions it quickly became clear that this man had lost whatever faith he had once had, since he usually waffled away with a few blessed thoughts, making no secret of his own personal doubts.

And at the same time of course we were surrounded by a completely alien culture with a multiplicity of different religious festivals and garishly decorated idols being carried around the streets, which inevitably left me reeling and confused.

Hinduism seemed to be a religion of such appalling hopelessness! The despair that I had first seen in the Calcutta slums pervaded the whole of life and could best be summed up in one single word 'fatalism'.

There is absolutely nothing that you can do about the terrible situation in which you now find yourself. Everything that you are suffering is a result of sins in your past life, and your only hope is patiently to endure what lies ahead of you - however terrible that might be in the vain hope that you might be reincarnated to something a bit higher up the caste system next time round.

Perhaps after several hundred reincarnations progressing painfully and slowly up the ladder of life, you might eventually be allowed to escape from all these terrible sufferings into the eternal oblivion that is Nirvana.

Needless to say this is the most effective recipe for despair that I have ever come across, and something that many people have not surprisingly reckoned to be the curse of India in its total lack of any glimmer of hope.

Corruption flourished everywhere from the highest to the lowest corners of the land, and no one seemed to see anything wrong with this. Hinduism has very little to do with honesty or reality as we were soon to discover. The 'real world' exists up above and anything on this earth is a poor shadowy imitation. Reality like suffering was therefore of no particular consequence.

Police would cheerfully frame our plantation workers for some crime unless they received the appropriate bribe; missionaries would often have to bribe to get their suitcases out of the docks; river dams and bridges would collapse at the first heavy rain because so much of the original cement had been adulterated for different people down the line to get their "cut", that there was no longer enough left to hold the structure together!

Powdered milk and blankets stamped by different aid organizations were regularly seen "for sale" in the markets of Calcutta - and meanwhile the poor and hungry had no one to defend and protect them and nobody to care.

It was about this time that Mother Theresa had been led to open her first Home for the Dying, and the simple caring love that could be seen daily at work within those walls was eloquent enough testimony at very least to a God who cared. Right next door stood the bloodthirsty temple of Kali where goats were sacrificed regularly, accompanied by the most spine chilling screams. This was certainly a real light in a very dark place.

Life in India certainly showed us clearly enough what a wonderful heritage our Christian tradition was, and the inestimable value of a faith that is historical and given by God to man - instead of searched for by man through the creative machinations of his own mind.

Gandhi himself is said to have told his followers, "If you want a guru then go to Jesus Christ". And on another occasion he told some expatriates, "If you had come to us living Christ then India would have become Christian overnight."

How terrible that we had been such dreadful witnesses to our faith down the years! In fact Indian Christians who travelled to the so called Christian countries of the West would often comment on how little we valued or lived out what we believed.

But with all this confusion of religions and so little spiritual input my faith was beginning to wear more than a little thin at the edges!

How much of God did I really know for myself? Indeed if this was all there really was to Christianity then most of the time it didn't really seem enough. When the bible spoke of "power" and "rivers of living water" then how did we ever find these in our own experience? Because personally I knew that my own river bed was very nearly dried up altogether!

Chapter Eleven

Love Never Received

Around this time our first child was born to us in Doom Dooma Plantation Hospital. Wonderful as we both found this event, it began to open up cracks in my own experience that I had never realized were there. All those years of childhood neglect now seemed to have left me with yet another gaping hole in my life.

As I surveyed this beautiful little creature lying in the cot beside me, my feelings were verging on panic! She would be helplessly dependent on me for every ounce of love and care, and in my conscious experience I hardly knew what that was - let alone how to give this.

What was this kind of love anyway? Perhaps in my earliest memories before my own parents had died I had known something of its real meaning, but for the rest of my life it seemed to me that others had only taken from me - and now I would need to be giving out all over again.

As we returned to England on leave that year I was feeling almost more empty and powerless than ever before. I knew I would have to look for help or sink without trace - but where would I find this and who could I ask?

As a respite from living with our respective parents whilst on leave from India we had sometimes taken refuge in the top flat belonging to London friends. Now as we returned there I took the risk of sharing with Gill a little of what I was feeling.

She had seemed particularly excited about something at the time, and I had noticed a new feeling of life and warmth about her. What she told me sounded amazing, but immediately I knew that this was what I needed more than anything.

Together with a number of friends they had recently discovered a new power and a new love in their lives. This was something that had always been promised in the bible, and written about in the Acts of the apostles, but for some reason the church had allowed it to remain dormant and unclaimed for many years - and indeed until recently many people had just assumed was only meant for the early days of the church.

The Holy Spirit was not just some mystical figure who came almost unrecognized into our lives when we first believed, but if we asked Him to He would fill us up with a new experience of his power and love that could completely transform our lives from within - just as the words of the Confirmation service promised.

She showed me the promise in Luke 11 verse 13. If you being evil know how to give good gifts to your children, how much more will your heavenly father give the Holy Spirit to those who ask him?

Well this certainly sounded like the very thing that I had been missing and I could hardly wait to find out.

As the day for our return drew closer I began to wonder if God would ever come to me in this way. By this time I was almost battering the doors of heaven and begging him to do something about my need before we had to leave again for the desolate emptiness of India.

At the end of the very last week a friend arrived at the flat to visit us, and half way through a cup of tea she suddenly announced that there was something she would have to say. "I do hope you don't mind Ann," she said rather apologetically, "but I think that God is wanting me to lay hands on you. Would that be alright do you think?"

Of course it sounded a bit strange, but by this time I really did not care what happened just so long as I could find this deeper experience of God in my life. Besides, the early apostles had "laid hands" on people who came to them so it sounded authentic enough.

Alone in an upstairs room as she prayed for me in a soft unrecognizable language, I felt the most extraordinary sense of God's love flowing through my body, together with an actual physical vibrant warmth. It seemed as if he was saying to me, "My child I really do love you, trust in me, believe in me."

I wanted to cry the feeling was so beautiful and so very much what I had needed all these years. As I would soon discover this love would have to be allowed to reach down into the empty caverns and all the pain of my early years, but that would come later.

When we returned to India this time it was as if a completely new dimension had been added to my life. Deep inside of me was a heart certain of the love and power of God that I had never known before.

"And I will give them an undivided heart and put a new spirit within them. I will remove from them their heart of stone and give them a new heart of flesh," says the prophet Ezekiel.

My faith was no longer just a matter of reason and argument, but just as the scriptures had promised, God had actually written this on my heart. And whereas previously talking about my faith had seemed a rather embarrassing thing to do, now suddenly the words just seemed to come almost as soon as I opened my mouth.

Sometimes I would be surprised to hear myself talking about a certain subject, only to find that this was the very thing that particular person had needed to hear.

In every other way our lives in India became even more difficult than they had been previously. Theoretically we were supposed to be living in Calcutta for the following year, but no sooner had we got ourselves settled into our new home there than Peter was sent back to Assam to sort out some pressing problem there.

I had really looked forward to being involved in 'life' again away from the very boring pointless social existence that usually goes on in remote colonial corners of the world. And of course in Calcutta there would have been endless opportunities to help out with refugee work and to do something about all that terrible poverty.

But within weeks were we back in Assam living in an unbelievably hot bungalow that had been officially condemned by the company many months previously. There were so many rats that we would lie in bed at night listening to them playing in the rafters directly above our heads, and on one occasion an enormous rat even jumped out at me as I opened the desk drawer!

73

In addition, I was pregnant again with a child who threatened to miscarry from the very beginning.

Humanly speaking there was not a lot to be said for these months back in Assam, but a new heart had certainly been given to me and if nothing else I was able to spend a lot of time listening to God.

We returned to Calcutta three months before Gina was born and just as the Naxalite riots were coming to a head. It was not even possible to risk staying in our own home as the day drew closer, since street mobs were throwing petrol bombs at any car that ventured out, and not even an ambulance could get through. In the end I just had to go and stay at the hospital.

Three months later we set sail for home together with our lovely new baby - and for what I hoped would be a much more fulfilling way of life.

But of course I did not realize how drainingly dependent two tiny children could be for twenty four hours a day - especially without that army of servants that I had unwillingly grown accustomed to!

Any thoughts about working or finding a creative input for my life were an absolute joke! All I could do was struggle to survive somehow amidst the seemingly endless chores of house work and child minding - and quite frankly it seemed to me that I had had to survive for far too many years of my life already.

Deep down I was beginning to feel quite bitter about everything that life had done to me, and memories that I had buried were beginning to surface at an alarming rate. I found myself resenting the childhood that I had never had, the endless demands that my parents and now the children were putting onto me, and the desperate boredom and pointlessness of life.

After that wonderful earlier experience of God's love all this really did not seem to make any sense. What was any of this worth if it only led to this kind of misery and depression afterwards?

I did try to tell Peter something of what I was going through, but there was little sympathy on offer from this direction.

"Good heavens - you're a British housewife now! Other people have to learn to cope with all of this, so you'll just have to do the same," he said, continuing to leave a trail of clothes and work around for the non-existent bearer to pick up!

Basically what he said was perfectly true, but as always there was a great deal more to what I was suffering deep down than the mundane more obvious things on the surface - though I could not have put words to these feelings at the time.

For a very brief period between going to university and in the BBC I had experienced small glimpses of what life could be like - those wonderful months when Patrick was still alive, the challenge of my work and the interest it had given me, and the early months of Peter and I falling in love and our engagement. But now it seemed that 'shades of the prison house' had closed around me for ever and this was all that life had to offer.

The impossible heaviness I now felt as I surveyed this desert stretching endlessly before me was almost more than I could bear. Sometimes I honestly felt that if I had not known first hand what a terrible legacy I would be leaving for Peter and the children I would have put an end to my life once and for all.

Only a few months after returning to England my adoptive father died very suddenly and unexpectedly and I was catapulted into a well of grief that I had never known existed. And underneath it all was a bottomless sea of grief about the death of my own father who had died so long ago and for whom I had never been allowed to grieve. I scarcely knew what to do the pain was so bad.

As I struggled to help my mother cope with what she was feeling I realized something else that was almost as hard to cope with. Now once again she would be totally and drainingly my responsibility.

It felt as if the most intolerable burdens had been loaded back onto my shoulders and no one in the whole wide world was willing to help me carry these.

So much for your promise that "your burden is easy and your yoke light," I stormed at the seemingly empty heavens! Will this nightmare never end?

Very shortly after this my neighbour's husband was killed in a plane crash and as a good neighbour I wanted to go round to comfort her - but my feet felt like lead as I struggled down the road. I really could hardly bear to face the pain she was feeling.

Gradually but inescapably I was beginning to catch glimpses of all the pain and hurt that lurked in the cellars of my life. Cracks were suddenly appearing that even I could not paper over, and yet what was I supposed to do about this?

What had happened to all this wonderful new experience of God's love and power I asked myself angrily? Things seemed even worse now than they had done before!

Chapter Twelve

A Shaky Facade!

Towards the end of that incredibly difficult first year back in England our vicar suddenly announced that he would be starting up a counselling group in the parish and I was one of the first people he invited to join this.

Whilst briefly studying psychology at university I had discovered how fascinating this whole field could be, and so I signed on quite enthusiastically. At least this would be something interesting that I could actually do since the whole course took place during the evenings.

Before we began in those first few weeks I thought of this mainly in terms of 'learning to help other people' since I had still not really begun to understand the full extent of my own problems.

But after this initial burst of interest and enthusiasm a huge wave of dread threatened to drown me without trace!

As we went further and further into the course there was no way that I could escape the pain that was reverberating in the cellars of my life. And what was even worse many of the role plays and exercises that the course contained were actually beginning to dredge up feelings that I could scarcely bear to face all over again - the rejection, the loneliness, the bereavement, the fear, and the ever present despair about life.

Often I would return home in the evening in floods of tears because of some terrible memory that had been resurrected by an exercise in the group, and naturally enough Peter was concerned that none of this was doing me any good at all.

"Why on earth do you keep on going?" he would ask in exasperation.

It was a valid question, and I honestly didn't know the answer! I suppose that deep down I knew that somewhere in these murky waters of my memory lay the reason for all the unhappiness I felt about life.

But of course this went against the standard British stiff upper lip attitude to life!

"What is past is past and better forgotten about." "Pull yourself together. Just pray about it and trust God and everything will be fine."

These were some of the 'helpful' comments dished out to me on the very rare occasions I risked talking about what I was going through with anyone outside the counselling world.

For most people who knew nothing of the deep emotional hurts that others often have to go through these were just glib easy phrases to roll off the tongue!

However, knowing about this with my mind was one thing - getting rid of the pain and despair was something else.

There wasn't even anyone in the counselling group that I felt I could share with although I am sure they tried. I heard from another friend in the parish later that the vicar had pronounced me 'totally out of reach'.

If I am honest I think I would have seen everyone around me as potential persecutors at this point in time. And consequently their willingness to help instead of harm me would really have had to be written in blood for me to actually believe this!

Years of bitter experience had long ago taught me that there was absolutely no one in the whole wide world that I could really trust with the full depths of my own hurt and rejection

The walls of 'apparent strength' and ability that I had so successfully constructed in years gone by were still holding somehow against all would be invaders - but now instead of protecting me from any further hurt they were actually preventing any chance of real healing in my life.

One of the exercises we were asked to try in the group produced some extraordinary results and revealed my true situation very graphically.

Shut your eyes, they told us, and try to imagine yourself as a tree. Take time to see exactly what that tree looks like. Are you tall and strong with good spreading branches reaching out to the sunlight, or do you feel somewhat shaky and fragile?

What are your roots like? Do they stretch down into the soil or do they feel shallow and insecure?

To this day I can still remember the sense of shock I experienced after dong this exercise, and I honestly think it would have been impossible to represent my situation more graphically in any other way.

From one angle the tree of my life looked pretty impressive. It was growing all by itself close to a deep river, and it was tall and leafy with plenty of branches spreading out to the sunshine. On every available resting place there seemed to be heavy birds perched, but my tree looked strong enough to carry them.

And then as I looked down for the roots the angle of my picture changed dramatically and I experienced a sinking feeling in the pit of my stomach.

From the side away from the river the tree had seemed to be firmly rooted, secure and growing well but here on the other side it was inconceivable that the tree could even remain standing.

The roots on this side straddled pathetically out into absolute nothingness, for the tree was perched on the very edge of a gigantic ravine. One gust of wind or a minor landslide seemed all that it would take to send the whole thing crashing down into the valley below.

One thing alone was keeping this tree upright and still alive at all. Reaching far away down the cliff face, going over and round the rocks, but still keeping a hold somehow was an enormous tap root that reached right down to the deep waters below. Any sustenance reaching my tree had to come from this source, for truly there was nothing else to keep it alive.

My subconscious was replaying my current life situation back to me - and telling me that I had absolutely no everyday support from anyone or anything since I trusted no one. But that the only real love and security I had experienced firsthand was still coming from those very early childhood years when my parents were still alive and from no other source.

I suppose it would have appeared to most onlookers at the time that I was a perfectly normal strong and "okay" human being. But I can recollect being in the hospital just after our youngest daughter was born, surrounded by flowers and cards from well-wishers laid out on every available surface. The doctor had just made some comment about what a lot of friends I had, whilst I found myself realizing with a sinking heart that not one single one of these 'friends' actually knew what the 'real me' was like - and I was certain that they would never accept me if they did!

My life was just like one of those film sets I had come to know so well as a child - looking good from the outside, but in reality behind the scaffolding a very shaky facade!

Finally as this terrible course at last ground to a halt I heaved an enormous sigh of relief! It was over and done with, and I had managed to keep going somehow, despite the pain. Now I could forget all about this - or so I imagined!

Knowing I had done a counselling course other friends began sending me people who needed help. But even as I took on these assignments I realized each time that there was a great deal more that needed healing in my own life.

It is very difficult to help another person towards wholeness until you have first received the necessary healing and encouragement and I most certainly had not!

Quite by chance towards the end of the following year I bumped into a friend who had been on the same course as me, and I simply could not believe the change in her.

At the end of that dreadful course we had all been offered the possibility of a third and more in depth year. And needless to say this was something that I of all people had not the slightest desire to continue with. However, in my case I had really needed to go on, whereas most of the others did not.

But Lillian, although she too had found those years difficult, had courageously determined to see the whole thing through to the very end. And now here she was standing right there in front of me very obviously and dynamically different. It was almost difficult to believe that she was the same person!

As we chatted and she enthused about the past year I found myself regretting for the first time that I had not persevered. Was it really possible that I could have shaken free of my past in the same way?

As I heard myself mutter something to this effect she suddenly dropped the bombshell in my lap.

"It's not too late you know. They're starting another third year group in Haslemere next month and Jenny is going along, you could even travel down together." As she saw my hesitation she suggested a compromise. "You could always go along to the first session and see what it's like. After all you know they will never put pressure on for you to continue if you don't want to."

As I heard myself agree the die was cast.

Chapter Thirteen

Breaking Down the Defences

This time we were really in at the deep end and there would be no more splashing about in the shallows!

The leader of this particular group was a hardy perennial with razor sharp insight who was not about to be fooled by the thickness of my defences however well guarded!

On that very first evening we were asked to go round the group sharing what little we could remember of our early lives. Apparently when it came to my turn I told the story of the death of my whole family in a totally detached way as if it had all happened to someone else a very long time ago.

Jenny said it sounded just as if I was a little girl as I spoke the words.

One of the group leaders turned to me in amazement and asked, "Don't you feel anything at all about that Ann? Personally I can tell you that I shan't be happy until I see you angry about everything that has happened to you!"

At the time I probably thought that was a very unhelpful remark and dismissed it out of hand. For many years I had just accepted all the bad things that had ever happened to me as just my lot in life. 'What can't be cured must be endured'. Put a brave face on it and keep on living somehow.

In the end I had simply shut out all the feelings until I could scarcely feel anything. In this way I had been able to survive somehow, just struggling on and hoping that things would get better one day.

What I did not realize until later that same year was the simple fact that shutting out pain shuts out all true enjoyment of life as well. If we protect ourselves with this kind of armour plating then all the good and happy feelings get barricaded away along with the bad ones, leaving us in a sort of twilight zone, unable to feel anything very much at all.

Just like an anaesthetic, this works quite well to protect the actual root of the pain, but it also reduces the whole person to a sort of zombie-like state, with very little awareness of genuine personal identity or emotion - except perhaps for very occasional quite unreasonable outbursts, usually about nothing very much!

I left the group that first night bewildered about all that had happened but still unconvinced about the anger - however I did not have long to wait!

It was extraordinary but as the weeks went by I DID become more and more angry about what I felt life was doing to me - but as so often happens with deeply buried hurts this appeared to be taking place at a 'now' level.

Today's events can also trigger yesterday's pain. After my adoptive father's death had opened the flood gates I had wept almost uncontrollably at the funeral of another close friend, to the clear amazement and horror of the very uptight British congregation around me in the graveyard!

If ever one of the children's pet animals died I could scarcely cope with their tears or very natural expressions of grief. Everything in me cried out against facing this deep searing pain that had lain dormant inside my fortifications for so many years until it had reached almost epic proportions.

But now suddenly on top of everything else Peter's job was taking him away for longer and longer periods leaving me to cope single-handed with the needs of three little children. But if I ever said anything he would become quite angry, telling me that I ought to understand that his job demanded this. And of course at one level he was absolutely right.

But deep down I was drowning in all those early childhood hurts - my father going off to die, my adoptive father leaving me to "look after" my mother whilst he went off with this other woman, and always the same thought...

"You have to understand; your mother needs you; the children need you..."

"What about me?" something deep inside of me was screaming. Can't any of you ever consider how all this is effecting me? Why must I always just "put up with" everything?

Why are all these other people's needs so much more important than anything I might be experiencing?

And anyway, what was I supposed to do with all these unacceptable emotions? Was this a Pandora's box that I had opened or was it the door to healing as so many on the counselling course had predicted?

Someone would need to help me to face up to the feelings that were now screaming for attention - that much was clear. Because even I had now understood that the clue to freedom almost certainly lay in facing up to all of these buried emotions.

Then one day, almost out of the blue, the fortifications of my life begun to finally crumble as two friends from the counselling group offered to come and help me work through some of these deeply buried hurts and memories. Their presence in helping me face up to all of this was invaluable and I really needed their loving prayer and support. I have no idea how long the session lasted, but we had gone back a long way into the mists of time and when it came to an end I felt totally and utterly exhausted.

But in some strange way I also felt more alive than I could ever remember feeling!

Up until this moment I had accepted each and every blow that life had dealt me with despairing passive resignation and as a result my whole horizon had become clouded with hopeless joyless dust - probably it had been like that for many years.

It was almost as if I had been drugged and conditioned to spend my life in hopeless subjection, but now that the anaesthetic was rapidly wearing off I was suddenly aware of a thousand different sensations.

On the one hand there was this whole wonderful awareness of life that seemed suddenly to bring everything out in glorious technicolour, almost as if I had never seen it before - the beauty of nature around me, the love of friends and family, the joy of small everyday happenings that had previously just washed over me.

But on the other hand of course was the very pain that the walls had originally been built to keep out. Thrown like a heavy blanket across the whole of my life there was now this thick layer of sorrow, so that at first I could only see everything through a mist of unending grief.

I cried over every sad book and film, over little things that would never have touched me at all, and now suddenly it seemed impossible for me to cope with the smallest problem without going off the deep end!

As I flooded my way tearfully through yet another box of tissues my poor husband could really not begin to understand what had happened to me. Emotions were something you scarcely ever talked about let alone expressed in this very embarrassing and un-British fashion!

"Goodness you have become so difficult these days - what on earth has happened to you?" he would protest as yet again I refused to meekly fall into line on cue as I had always done before.

But the extraordinary thing was that I really had no idea that all this was down there. It had effectively been shut out and could only have been recognized by what psychiatrists would call my body language - the fact that I had always seemed so depressed, and was constantly tired. The tension my body was under as it struggled to cope somehow with the emotional pain of years.

In the words of T S Eliot's chorus from "Murder in the Cathedral" it was as if I had been living and partly living for many years.

Chapter 14

The Spiral Staircase

These memories were written down nearly twenty years ago and have lain gathering dust on a cupboard shelf until I rediscovered them whilst moving house. Re-reading them now after all this time it is hard for me to even recognize the unhappy depressed person I probably was at that time.

But it would be wrong to imply that the pain of the past had miraculously disappeared altogether leaving me completely free of any scar tissue.

The most helpful comparison I have heard for people with very painful childhood memories is that of ascending a spiral staircase. The higher up you go the further away you will travel from all that childhood trauma, but as the staircase continues on up and round it will almost certainly bring you back again to a different view of the same painful experiences. Certainly they will be more distant this time round, but they still have the same power to reactivate very similar needs and feelings.

For several years after these early chapters I lived on a sort of comfortable plateau enjoying the family, getting involved with an ever widening circle of friends and interests - all of which began to fill up the gaping chasm of that terrible empty ravine.

By this time I was taking part in a regular late night television program with people like Adrian and Bridget Plass, heavily involved with the Church of England Newspaper, and editing the company magazine amongst many other interesting projects - but then quite suddenly, and out of the blue, our whole world fell apart dragging me back once again to an alarmingly similar view of the traumas of my past life.

At the height of the 1980s recession Peter lost his job through a stock market takeover and we were suddenly out trying to survive somehow living on the dole. Although a qualified accountant, nearly all of his work had been involved with the management of tropical plantations in different corners of the world, so that trying to find a UK based job in a raging recession like that one proved absolutely impossible for someone with his kind of work experience.

After eighteen months of job hunting it became clear that until and unless things improved significantly on the home front there would be nothing available for him here in England. Deep down I think we both knew that this situation would very probably involve some kind of overseas posting.

With a great deal of trepidation Peter finally accepted a job managing a group of eighteen plantations scattered all over the islands of Papua New Guinea - or in other words about as far away as one could possibly go! And although this meant leaving everyone and everything behind us I felt it was vitally important to go with him to provide some kind of support.

With heavy hearts we took the children out of local schools and arranged for them to board wherever we could find reasonable places, and then proceeded to pack up and leave our whole world behind us. Even the dog had to be boarded out with local friends.

It would not have taken a genius to predict that this particular turn of the staircase would reveal a view of many really painful early memories which I had optimistically imagined were now well and truly behind me.

Many aspects of our life on the far shores of the Pacific were really delightful - a house right on the sea facing the setting sun, friendly outspoken Australian neighbours, barbecues on the beach and local friends whose faith was really infectious - but all of this was of course a million miles away from the busy life that I had known and been very much a part of in England.

Worst of all for us was the separation from our children who were constantly in our thoughts and prayers, but still many thousands of miles away. The Company would fly them out for school holidays but as these precious weeks drew to a close I increasingly faced their departure with absolute dread.

Such a situation would probably have been very difficult for anyone, but for me it brought me yet again close to the edge of all that wretched childhood bereavement.

One very real compensation was that at least this quiet life by the sea proved an excellent opportunity to finally get down to some serious writing since there was very little else to occupy my time on the island. I soon managed to positively zip through several ideas for books that I had been stockpiling for some time, writing five books in the five years that we were there - something which I would certainly never have achieved during my busy life in England.

By the end of that time a whole series of things began to change very dramatically in our world - a revolution in Bouganville had suddenly put half of our plantations out of action for the foreseeable future, the volcano above the town where we were living was threatening to erupt again, and more important than anything it was becoming obvious that the family really needed us living back at home again as they had now almost finished with school and university.

We were both thrilled to be going back, and word on the grapevine was that the whole job situation in England had now significantly improved. Although sad to be saying goodbye to our tropical island and the many friends that we had made there, I don't think it ever occurred to either of us to wonder how we would cope with returning home to England and to the life that we had once known.

Both in the Foreign Office and on the Mission Field the problems of returning home even after just two or three years posting are well documented. But we were both strangely unprepared and had naively imagined that we would be able just to take up our old lives again exactly where we had left off.

How wrong can you be?

Inevitably, five years on a remote tropical island is to say the least a life changing experience! Moreover, returning to life back home after such a long gap inevitably meant that we were now seriously out of touch - although I don't think either of us had really appreciated this.

Life back home in rainy dark old England could scarcely hold a candle to the tropical beaches and technicolour underwater world of our island. The locals seemed pleased to see us, but inevitably they had got used to living without us around - and instead I found myself missing the many really deep friendships we had made with people who were now many thousands of miles away.

And worst of all having had to leave the children behind in boarding school and university for so many years, our return coincided fairly exactly with the time when they would soon be setting off on their own, having reached the age when they were ready to fly the family nest. They needed us at home to help with all of this, but they would soon no longer be around for us to enjoy.

The view from my spiral staircase now mirrored fairly exactly the most traumatic events in my childhood that I had naively imagined were well behind me. And it only took one or two other local problems to threaten to tip me right over the edge, unable to stop crying and alarmingly close to a breakdown.

I was having coffee with a close friend from our church and sharing what little I felt able to, when she announced that that she was going down the very next day to see her own counsellor who might possibly be able to help me deal with what was happening.

Mary proved to be the most remarkable woman and an absolute life line for many years to come. Paralyzed by polio in her late teens and unable to take up the career she would have chosen, she had dedicated her whole life to counselling and helping others. As a quadriplegic imprisoned in a wheelchair and needing a carer to get her through the most mundane tasks of every day life, she was really an amazingly courageous person and just who I needed to get me to finally deal with the memories that were still haunting me.

Whilst we were away in Papua New Guinea, my adoptive mother had finally died leaving me free at last to deal with some of the ravages of living with her terrible temper and her treatment of me down the years. Besides which, I now at last felt free to set out to discover more about my own real parents and the kind of person I was created to be instead of the very ill-fitting straight jacket into which my adoption had crammed me for all those years.

For much of the time we worked with dreams which I found absolutely fascinating. It was amazing how this dream language, well documented in the bible, could take me back down the years and into memories of much happier early times, but also how they could speak into a now situation.

The first significant dream that I could remember was of wandering around some uncomfortable rambling institution trying to find a place where I could actually belong. But however many doors I opened there was absolutely no room at all for me anywhere. Eventually I found myself going downstairs (into the subconscious) to search for somewhere. The dark and gloomy stairs descended into the depths of the building beneath a string of Christmas tree lights where every singe bulb had gone out.

In another dream I was searching around an old world village looking for a place where I had once belonged, but however much I tried this proved totally impossible because someone had built a gigantic railway track right through the middle of this lovely old place completely obscuring any recognizable landmarks.

It was becoming clear, even from my dreams, that like most adopted children I too needed to trace anyone left from my own birth family and thus to discover my real roots and where I belonged. But since my adoptive parents had done their best to choke off any distant relations who had attempted to stay in touch after my parents died, the search proved so difficult that I almost gave up the attempt.

In my adoptive mother's effects I discovered an old address for the cousin on my father's side who was somewhere in Eastern Australia, but on my mother's side the trail had really gone cold. I knew that they lived in South Africa and that my godmother had decided that in wartime it was simply not safe to send me out to live with them. I knew also that my adoptive mother had become very angry when they attempted to stay in touch and had eventually managed to choke them off ... but all I had to go on was an old dog-eared photograph which I had found in my adoptive mother's files of three young cousins who would of course be grown men by now.

There was also a letter from their mother saying how much she was longing to see me again once the war was over and travel was once again possible. But how would I find them all these years later?

None of the usual searches from the Mormon lists to the Salvation Army records showed up anything remotely helpful, and writing to the last known address on a letter in my 'mother's' files also predictably drew a complete blank. But then a friend came up with what sounded like a bizarre suggestion - that of getting in touch with Debretts.

To my amazement the answer came back almost by return giving the exact names and addresses of all three cousins, but telling me that their mother had already sadly died.

The letter left me feeling totally shell-shocked but hugely excited at one and the same time, and as a result we started making plans to visit South Africa as soon as reasonably possible. However, as the time for our visit drew closer, I began to experience a surprising amount of anxiety - probably like any adopted child preparing to meet their own real family for the first time.

Would they like me? Would they even want to see me? Did they actually know of my existence?

It was an extraordinary feeling that somewhere out there were some close flesh and blood relatives who I had not seen since I was a tiny child, but who must surely have something in common with me.

I made contact with them by letter, and it was obvious from the outset that my adoptive parents' tactics for banning them from my life had really worked, because as a result my aunt had never even told them of my existence. However, they sounded very warm and welcoming and immediately made plans for us to come. Though I imagine that at this stage they had absolutely no idea of what a big deal this would be for me!

By the time we reached Johannesburg at the end of a three week visit my anxiety level about this meeting had gone into orbit, and in the end Peter had almost had to drag me to my cousin's house. The closer it got the more scary the whole idea became for me - what on earth did I think I was doing!

But, of course, when we finally made contact all my fears and anxieties just evaporated and I immediately felt as much a part of them as if I had known them all my life. It was extraordinary and felt somehow as if the tent pole of my existence had finally found its true foundation - a family where I actually belonged.

Long after we returned home I found myself wanting to call them and to stay more in touch than distance allowed, and indeed we quickly started to make plans to return the following year.

But even before the year was out tragedy struck our own lives once again which made everything else seem trivial in comparison.

Just before Christmas, and only months after Peter's retirement, he was diagnosed with terminal cancer which the doctors had failed to diagnose despite innumerable visits to the surgery. It seemed such a cruel blow, especially as his parents had lived on well into their eighties. And as I struggled to help him cope with all that terrible treatment coming closer and closer to the end of his life, for me the very last thing I needed or expected was to have to live on without him around.

Chapter 15

Re-Owning the Past

Nearly seven long years had dragged by since Peter's death, and I had gradually rebuilt my life on the ashes of the past and with the help of many wonderful friends who had stayed alongside me. Now I had moved right away and started life all over again in the exciting city of Oxford.

That Christmas I travelled out to visit my daughter in Sydney and to meet my lovely new grandchild there for the first time. A friend had lent me her flat above Sydney harbour for a few months so I decided to stay on over in Australia and visit a whole lot of friends from our time in Papua New Guinea. It was at this point in time that I discovered that my cousin John was still alive and living just a few hours away.

Even just thinking about going to visit him made me quite apprehensive, so I had left the whole suggestion very much on hold.

After Christmas a friend and I had planned to go up to the beaches north of Sydney, but then to our surprise we found that every single resort in that area was already fully booked. Our only remaining choice was to head down to the Southern Highlands - which as it happened was extraordinarily close to where cousin John was living!

Even then I hesitated until the very end of that week and only hours before I had to leave to return to Sydney. But finally I took my courage in both hands and rang to see if he would be free the next day. The die was cast.

He was sitting in the corner of a darkened room when I finally reached the village. A recent car accident had obviously made it impossible for him to move around or even to get up to greet me, so we sat in the shadows and talked whilst his daughter fetched the tea.

It seemed very sad after all these years to have found him so badly injured, and as we talked I searched for some familiar memory of the big cousin I had known so long ago.

We must have talked for hours with scarcely a break and gradually I began to discover the man he had become. By some extraordinary coincidence he had also worked for many years managing a plantation in India, and it was clear that he still loved that country.

After this the family had moved to Australia, where he had worked for some time in Welfare, but then eventually bought his own farm which had proved a wonderful place to raise their five children. His wife Joan had died in tragic circumstances some five years ago, and he had sold their farm to come to this retirement village just to look after her in those last few painful years.

Well we certainly had plenty of experiences to share along those lines.

But as we talked something very strange began to happen. The years began to slide away and we both experienced an extraordinary sense of comfort and peace.

Now for the first time I heard about how traumatic he had found it when I was removed from his parents' home to be adopted away from the family. For a long time he had been completely unable to forgive his mother for not adopting me, and had apparently found it impossible to forget a neighbour's account of my despairing cries as I was almost dragged away from their home.

Only a few months previously when narrating family history to a grandchild he had found that he could not even talk about me because it was all still too painful. I found this extraordinarily comforting to know because I had felt so alone at that time.

Amazingly I discovered that he was also a believing Christian and on top of our deep rooted family connection this immediately gave us a wonderful bond. It seemed that we loved many of the same kind of things - and despite everything he still had that wonderful sense of humour which I remembered so well.

This unplanned last minute visit could only be a lightning stopover and I was due in Canberra the very next day.

As he came out to the car to say goodbye to me balanced precariously on two crutches, I felt sad to be leaving him, but strangely reinforced by a sense of belonging that had been missing all my life.

Would he stay in touch this time? Only time would tell!

His presence stayed with me long after I left the country to return to the freezing cold of England in late February.

I found myself wanting to tell people about how we had met up again after all these years and how surprisingly well we had got on together. There seemed to be some kind of deep family bonding going on that I couldn't explain - maybe he was like my father or maybe we just had the same genes? It hardly seemed possible that I had only been with him twenty four hours.

I sent him a copy of one of my books, and before I knew it he had started collecting everything else I had ever written from the internet websites. And after that the emails started coming, every day - and sometimes two or three times a day.

Dear Ann,
You truly are the icing on my latter years. I have just obtained a copy of 'Free to be Myself.' I had to go into Canberra today so took your book with me and this one really touched me.

I haven't read much, but already in the first few pages my eyes were filling with tears. It was quite extraordinary. This is so much the kind of thing I would love to have written myself.

Dear Ann,
Do you happen to remember the day I took you to the Zoo? This recollection has always stayed with me....
"With her mother's energy she slipped away like an eel through the surrounding crowds. Frustrated, I found myself stuck on the perimeter. She could not be reached....The girl with the happy, shining face stood within a few feet of the monkey.... I was petrified that she might touch the netting. I could do nothing.

97

The monkey was spitting at all and sundry. The crowd retreated, except for one small girl. With a laughing face, she stood her ground. And then she spat back.
I was horrified... "

How extraordinary John! There is something very familiar about all of this hidden deep in my subconscious, but I couldn't honestly say that I could "remember" the occasion, and no doubt it has got mixed up with numerous visits to the zoo with my own children... Spitting back at the monkey - well I guess I have needed that strength just to survive what was thrown at me later!

It's a really comforting thought that you can remember me as a child - even if I did horrify you by spitting at the monkey! I know how much my own children love to hear stories of what they did when they were little, but of course for me that has just never been possible.

Incidentally I don't mind in the slightest being called S.I. - especially now that I know that it means 'sugar icing'.
Look after yourself, love Ann

My dear S.I. Cousin.
Today I suddenly realized that your courage in coming to Yass has actually released all the hidden tensions about you being shut out by my family.
Thank you Ann.... You have no idea of the joy you have released within me.

My memory often reverts to your playing with the cat in our house... Your face was wreathed in smiles as you explained that 'Blitz' preferred yellow knitting needles. ('Blitz' was so called because during the bombing he would chase up the curtains).
Well here it is now 9.45pm I am off to bed with your book of 'Confessions'...I only read a few pages before turning out the light...Luv JOHN

Dear John,
How are you getting on? I hope the acquisition of some of my books hasn't weighed you down with all that reading!? I don't think any of those are particularly brilliant, so please don't feel you have to plough through them on my account!

Do hope the leg is progressing well and you are getting around a bit better? I suppose it is nearly autumn there now, and at long last we are getting a few possible glimpses that Spring may be on the way. Ducks are flying round the pond over the road looking for somewhere to nest (they actually laid an egg in my garden last year!) and someone said they had a few daffodils out in their garden - though I certainly haven't seen any yet.

God bless and take care of yourself,   love from your S.I. cousin Ann

Dear S.I. Ann...

Do you remember 'Brief Encounter'?   It was a rather slow-moving film, but the essence of the story was the profound effect that a few hours could have on a chap like me....and I must confess how much I am enjoying your friendship.

With Love to my S.I. cousin. JOHN

My dear Ann (or today may I call you Celia Johnson?)

I am taking myself in hand. I had been consoling myself that the peace of mind you have given to me was because of the healing of old family wounds. Then last Sunday Narelle, a very young grandmother who cares for me as a daughter, came to lunch with some of her brood.

Afterwards she phoned and asked the reason for my having looked the happiest she had ever seen, which really made me think.
It is true that since my accident last September I have had a tremendous renewal in my faith but since December I seem to have an extra burst of energy. Though maybe this is just because I so look forward to printing out any of your emails that have come in. I am just like a teenager!

Our time together on 30th December has certainly had a deep effect on me and I am told it is perfectly normal for clients to fall in love with their 'therapists'!!
Ann despite my being so frank, I hope that we can continue writing.....

Thank you for being such a friend.....Love John
Dear Ann....It is 7.30am...

I meet many widows in this village. Some I know well enough to have a meal with or go searching for wild quinces, but they are just normal companions. None gave me the Zap which I received on the 30th December.

Actually the shock did not really register until Narelle asked me why I seemed so happy. Then everything fell into place. It was like watching crystals form. Suddenly my eyes began to see the real beauty of life.

On and on this extraordinary flow of emails continued, crisscrossing the world and shrinking the thousands of miles that separated us. But as I am sure readers will understand I need to draw a veil over most of what followed.

It was not long before he was asking me to marry him, and suddenly I urgently needed to draw back from the brink.

He was nearly ten years older than me and I had promised myself after those terrible years of Peter's final illness and death, that I would never even consider marrying again - and certainly not someone so much older where there was any likelihood of the same nightmare repeating itself. I simply could not bear to even think about this.

But at the same time I was desperate not to lose this very special relationship with my long lost cousin, and even thinking about the possibility of this made me want to cry from the very depths of my being. If only he lived in the same country or at the very least on the same continent and not twelve thousand miles away.

As we struggled to cope with this situation it was clear that we were both longing to spend more time with each other, but what would be the best way to do this? We considered India because at least it was half way between us and we both knew the country well, but in the end the obvious solution seemed for him to come over to the UK and take a look at my world. Finally it was arranged that he would come and spend a whole month with me in England that summer.

I made only one condition for the visit - that there should be absolutely no further mention of that dreaded eight letter word 'marriage'.

Chapter Sixteen

A New Beginning

As the day dawned for his arrival at Heathrow I became more and more apprehensive about what on earth I had let myself in for. We had communicated so well by email but how would we get on in real life - and for four whole weeks?

Not for the first time I seriously began to doubt my own sanity!

His welcoming smile quite literally enveloped me when we met up, but he was so much more disabled than I had fully realized, because, as I soon discovered, the series of car accidents went back a long way and had nearly finished him off more than once!

Apparently my mother had observed this tendency in him many years ago when she had refused to let him even push my pram!

But in some strange way the sheer strength of his personality and the love and warmth that he exuded made you overlook this in no time at all. It was fascinating to watch this in action as he met up with so many of my friends. I could see that people really warmed to him right away, and of course it was very easy for me to introduce him as my long lost cousin rather than just some man I had met on the other side of the world!

Amazingly those four weeks seemed to simply fly past whilst we found so many things we really enjoyed doing together. I had been an amateur painter for many years and now I discovered how much he really enjoyed coming out sketching with me and drinking in the beauty of the countryside. Since neither of us could walk very far this naturally proved a brilliant alternative to exploring on foot.

The history and beauty of Oxford fascinated him, and the warm gold stone of the Cotswold villages just down the road were an endless source of delight. A week after he arrived we went down to stay in Devon exploring many of the haunts that I had come to know and love, from the wonderful rocky harbours and open seascapes to the dramatic crags and misty moorland of Dartmoor.

Another time we found ourselves in Cambridge and I was able to show him where we had lived during those last few years before my parents died and to visit their grave together. It was extraordinary for me to fully appreciate, perhaps for the first time, that my parents were also his very own aunt and uncle - and above all to discover how much he had loved and respected my father.

We seemed to feel completely at ease in each other's company, laughing at all the same things, and talking for hours but enjoying the silences as well.

As the time for his departure came round it was hard for me to believe that we could possibly have been in each other's company for four whole weeks.

He had been true to his promise not to bring up that dreaded eight letter word 'marriage', but this remained very much the 'elephant in the room' - and he would occasionally just let slip an oblique reference to the 'forbidden subject'!

In the meantime, since I had not changed my mind on this subject, I saw absolutely no reason to tell anyone else about this. With the exception of one or two very close friends who had happened to be staying when he first started asking me to marry him, hardly anyone knew about this - and certainly not my own family!

Years of working as a counsellor had taught me to be very wary of what others might think or of allowing them the opportunity to influence me on such a very personal subject. It was my life and I was the one who would have to live with my decision! I could see that my family and friends really liked this 'long lost cousin' - and without a doubt there was this very deep family connection going back down the years which gave me a wonderful sense of belonging - but to actually marry the man would of course be something altogether different!

As we said our goodbyes he told me he would be writing from his son's place in Hong Kong to propose to me one more time.

Right up until I left him at the airport I had not once considered the possibility of changing my mind on this subject - it was just a bridge too far and the ramifications seemed far too difficult, so there was an end to the matter!

However, I had reckoned without the huge empty space that his departure would leave behind him. It seemed that his presence and his personality had filled the house and it was no time at all before I realized that I really did not want to live on there without him around - especially as he would soon once again be twelve thousand miles away from me.

No amount of visits down under or overseas holidays could possibly compensate for the wonderful day to day relationship we had discovered together, and it became obvious that as a close friend had said to me, "God would never have brought us together at this time in our lives if he had not meant it for something more."

That weekend as I went down to stay with friends in Winchester, I realized that despite all my earlier reservations I could now only say "Yes" to his proposal - however complicated the outcome would almost certainly be - and however much of a shock to my family and friends, most of whom had not the slightest idea that this was even a possibility!

When you are already in your seventies and eighties there is not a lot of point in hanging around as time can be at a premium!

We were not planning some elaborate first time white wedding but just a small gathering of friends who had actually met him and who we knew would be happy to celebrate the occasion with us. Coming from the other side of the world it was obvious that not many of his own family and friends would be able to make the occasion, though wonderfully just a few did.

In honour of the India connection we used a rickshaw to travel to and from the church, which had the added advantage of being able to come right up the aisle and rescue John from having to hobble down this after the service!

As long as we are able we plan to spend part of the year in the UK and part in Australia, whilst getting our extended families together for the very first time. My children had of course never known any of my real family and now they have five step-brothers and sisters, and we share seventeen grandchildren between us!

As Helen Keller once said, "Life is either a daring adventure or it is nothing at all!"

So despite age and disability we are both just trusting God for the future.

Postscript

My first contact with Ann as a tiny baby was tinged with disappointment. I was so excited to find that her large wheeled pram could generate great speed when I pushed this! But her mother was very fearful of an accident and I was quickly sacked as her personal chauffeur.

I suspect that even then Ann must have been quietly listening in, as today she equates this early lack of driving ability with my rather frequent car accidents in later life!

At the age of six her mother was dying and for a time Ann came to live with us. I must confess that when I was sixteen I really loved my little smiling fair haired cousin. The picture of her playing with the cat 'Blitz' is still vividly imprinted on my mind all these years later.

London soon became too dangerous, and Ann returned to Cambridge, but within a very short time both of her parents had died from cancer. So she once more returned to our home, this time to be adopted by my family. The joyful day arrived but sadly I was late back from school because I had a Saturday detention. Afterwards I rushed home to greet my beloved cousin - but when I got home there was silence. She had already left.

At the very last moment my mother had changed her mind and refused to take Ann in to live with us. It still hurts me when I recall being told by a neighbour about Ann's terrible cries as she was dragged away to an unknown destination.

I could neither understand nor forgive my mother's lack of compassion and as soon as possible I left home to join the Army. But before the call-up papers arrived I found myself at a scout camp close to where Ann had been adopted. I phoned her new parents and managed to arrange a visit.

It was really great to meet up with her again, but the door was very quickly closed against any further contact. The following morning my father received a call at his law firm, making it quite clear that Ann had been adopted as a "clean skin", (an Australian term for a person who has no family connections). The instructions were very clear that we were no longer to have any part in her life.

After four years military service I turned my back on England. For ten years I worked in India, happily married to my first wife Joan who was a teacher out there. Then when it became politically the right time for Europeans to leave, we settled in Australia.

Our five children grew up healthy and strong and they all doing well. After I retired and my first wife Joan had sadly died, I started to write up our family history. To my amazement when I reached the part about Ann, I found that the memories were still so painful that I could not even put pen to paper.

Several years later I received that phone call out of the blue from Ann, saying that she was visiting her daughter in Sydney and wanted to find out more about her real family. The rest as they say is history!

It is as if that early love for my cousin has blossomed once again and we both have been really happy together after all those years apart.

John